JESUS, LOVER, OF MY SOUL

"WITHDRAWAL SYMPTOMS"

BY

BARBARA L. BREWER LINDSEY

Jesus, Lover of My Soul

Copyright © 2008

Barbara L. Brewer Lindsey

ISBN: 978-0-9787739-1-5

Dedication

I honor God, my Father, and His Son, Christ, Jesus, who gave me this talent. I dedicate this book to all those who are struggling to live a life of victory. God wants you to know He is on your side and with Him all things are possible.

I dedicate this book in memory of my Father and Mother the late George L. & Ella W. Brewer and the Brewer Family. I dedicate this book to my nephews, Paul A. Harris and the late William M. Harris, and my two nieces Ella Kay Harris Williams, & Deborah J. Harris and a host of family and friends.

I dedicate this book to my spiritual leaders: Pastors, Apostle Larry N. Crosby and Co-Pastor Sarah D. Crosby who is yet pouring the Spirit of Christ in me these thirteen years. A special thanks to my spiritual parents, in the Gospel, Apostle A.J. Jackson, and my spiritual mother, Pastor, Lizzie Jackson who poured the Spirit of Christ in me for eighteen years. A special dedication to the memory of two dear mothers in Christ: My mentor, the late "Dr. Annie Green, Vaughn", and my friend the late "Missionary Nelia White." I dedicate this book in memory of the late Josiah Brewer, my beloved grandson, who I will see again in heaven.

Acknowledgements

Special thanks, to Mr. Woody and "Woody's Printing and Copier Shop in Laurinburg, N. C. Special thanks to the staff, and Ms. Donna for her expertise in graphic designs who designed the covers of my books "Yielding Your Will Totally to God" and "Jesus, Lover, of My Soul."" I'm indebted to my spiritual father, Apostle A.J. Jackson, for his many teachings and quotes. I acknowledge one of his many quotes in my first book "Yielding Your Will Totally to God" on page seven as a quote from Apostle, Dr. A.J. Jackson PhD. Three kinds of people... Those that make it happen, those who watch it happen, and those who ask what happen?
I acknowledge (Dr.) Pastor Thomas of True Victory for her quote: Salvation is not the overall cure all in both my books of "YIELDING YOUR WILL TOTALLY TO GOD" and "JESUS, LOVER, OF MY SOUL."
Special thanks to Deacon W. Tillman who took the time to proof read this work. To all those who helped support and promote my first book: "Yielding Your Will Totally to God." Daily Journal, Editor, Kimberly Harrington, Rockingham, N.C., The Church Bulletin, Wadesboro, N.C.; and Apostle Lonnie & Dr. Queen Esther Sessoms Jr., Fayetteville, N.C. Special thanks to the saints of "Haven of Truth World Wide Deliverance Churches INC.", and friends and family for their support.

Table of Contents

Introduction

This book is written to every believer and to everyone whom is thinking about becoming a believer, but they are afraid of backsliding. When I'm witnessing to someone who hasn't receive Christ the thing that is foremost in their mind is what do I do with all the desires, passions, and appetites that comes from my soul?   So they say, when I stop doing this or that I'll get saved.

Sinner, I must inform you that you can't stop doing what you are doing in your own strength. (Zech.4:6) We have no power within ourselves to live a holy life that's why it took Jesus to die on the cross to pay for our sins and rise again the third day for our justification. Here is another statement I hear a lot when I'm witnessing "When I get ready I'll get saved." We can't come to Jesus when we get ready it's the Spirit of God that draws us to Christ Jesus. (John 6:44)

Many believers have fallen from grace because they didn't count up the cost. I have been a Christian now going on thirty-four years and thirty-three of those years I have been a single woman. I will share with you some of my most intimate testimonies that will witness the keeping power of the Holy Ghost.

Have you ever been in a church service and heard someone give a testimony that says, "I don't need no man because, JESUS is all I need." Mostly it's the sisters who don't have a mate or who have been hurt by a man at some point in their life that makes this type of confession. They are trying to medicate their pain by confessing "All they need is JESUS." I'm sorry to inform you "Jesus the Lover of my Soul" is not that kind of book. Personally I have walked with God for thirty-three years as a single woman and He has supplied all my need, but I never made that confession-that all I need is the Lord.   Marriage is the most inmate relationship between a man and woman next to the relationship that we have with God. God ordained marriage and gave Eve to Adam when Adam didn't even know he had a need. God knows what we need and He knows what's best for us so get healed and go on and serve the Lord with gladness. This advice goes to the males also we are by no mean prejudice. This book is to help you understand that only God can fill the void in your life. Husbands and wives don't look for your mates to fill that void. When we dedicate our life to Christ we have to go on to know the Lord whether we are single or married.

We must pray one for another and let the devil know we will not tolerate him making a mockery of the church. No longer will we see our sisters and brothers crucify our Lord, and Savior, Jesus, afresh by putting Him to an open shame with their raggedy lives. (Heb. 6:6) There are many sins of the works of the flesh that we deal with every day, but we must believe that God can keep us from yielding to the appetites and desires of the flesh. (Galatians 5:23; I Corinthians 6:18) Remember saints if Jesus die for you to be saved, He also rose again so you can stay saved. Philippians 1:6 says, "Being confident of this very thing, that he which hath begun a good work in you will perform it until the day of Jesus Christ."

Chapter 1

Abide in your Calling

(Testimony)

June, nineteen-seventy-eight, I gave my heart (life) to Jesus and He is the best thing that has happened to me. I was twenty-eight years young and I was married to Julius Lindsey for two years before I was born-again. My husband and I had been married two years now, but he hadn't given his heart to Christ. Elohim, began teaching me how to sanctify my husband by the life I lived. I Corinthians 7:14 - "For the unbelieving husband is sanctified by the wife, and the unbelieving wife is sanctified by the husband: else were your children unclean; but now are they holy."
I want to add that this was my second marriage and I was going to do everything that I could to make this marriage work. We were having problems before my conversion because my husband was an alcoholic. He was a kind-hearted man when he was sober, and I believe he loved his stepson, George, and I as much as he knew how to love us.

Elohim was teaching me to cook my dinner on Saturday night so there wouldn't be any complaints from my husband when I stayed in church a long time on Sunday. I was learning as a babe in Christ how to submit to my husband and love him so he could see Christ in me. The Potter (God) began to refine my character by shaping and molding me through much suffering. I praise God for the work He has done thus far, but He's not through with me yet!
 I was a babe in Christ during this time saved now about four to six months and Satan declared war against my marriage. He didn't care how long I was saved his best strategy was to hit hard while I was still a babe in Christ. I hadn't grown enough to have the knowledge that I needed to fight the enemy, but that was then and this is now!

Someone came to my home and began to talk to me about "Adultery." Now they didn't have all the information they needed or they believe that way at the time. They never told me why they was talking to me about "Adultery", but that God hated it, and if I didn't think I could talk to my husband about leaving the home they offered to talk to him for me. I told them that wouldn't be necessary I would talk to him, because I wanted to be saved, and I didn't want anything to separate me from God. In the back of my mind I thought maybe they was talking about my first marriage because many people believed that if your first husband was alive you were committing adultery even if you had gotten a divorce.

I found out years later they didn't know I had gotten a divorce and remarried in 1976. I want to add I got a divorce because my former husband was unfaithful and that's putting it lightly, and I did this before I gave my life to Christ Jesus. Later I will write a book on marriage and remarriage before and after salvation. We must learn how to rightly divide the word of truth. (II Tim. 2:15)

I apologized to my husband for marrying him, and having to hurt him by asking him to leave. I explained to my husband about the conversation that I had with this person, and I told my husband although this was hurting me that I didn't want to live in sin. I told my husband with all the strength that I had-I wanted to be real for God. My husband pleaded with me not to separate from him nor listen to them because they were wrong. I didn't listen because I thought I was doing the right thing. I filed for separation papers and had him to sign an agreement not to see me or come on the property where I lived. He signed the agreement October 18, 78. He would call me from his job and he pleaded with me to take him back many times, but one day he stopped calling. Almost a year later I heard my husband remarried and had move to Charlotte, NC. I filed for divorce six years later and it became final November 19, 84. I never heard from him again until his aunt told me he died in 2006.

In the space of four-months to a year of my conversion I

went from a married state to a single state. I enjoyed the benefits that came with marriage and I surely missed being held by my husband. Paul, the Apostle, began to write in I Corinthians 7:20 "Let every man abide in the same calling wherein he was called." I was called in a married state, but because of misunderstanding in less than a year I was single. In my eighth year of salvation God dealt with me and showed me what had happened. I went to this person for closure and I talk to them about what God showed me and they confessed that they didn't know we were married. They apologized to me and made a comment concerning my husband that was true, but I knew God could have delivered him.

I want to take this time to say to the saints of God, whatever your position that God has placed you in the body of Christ: first get all the facts or right information, and then be led by the Spirit of God before you tell someone to leave or stay with their spouse. I had two choices to make in my life at this point of my conversion: I could have chosen to be bitter with them or chosen to be better. I chose to be better and I forgave them for their mistake.

I said earlier that I enjoyed the benefits of marriage and now I found myself in a single state. Now I must go on to know the LORD to see what His purpose and plan is for my life. Marriage might be down the road later on but, I had to abide in my calling according to God's word and it didn't matter how I got there. Now I must trust God to keep what I have committed unto Him. One day I walked through the house, and said out loud to God: Well! I don't have a husband so I can't have sex. Oh! Oh! She is a minister of the Gospel and she said the word "Sex" she's not in the Spirit. To all the religious Pharisees, and Sadducees out there the word "Sex" isn't a bad word. God ordained marriage and sex was one of the benefits that God gave Adam and Eve. It wasn't just to replenish the earth it was a beautiful way for a husband and wife to express their love toward one another. God doesn't have to apologize for sex or for giving both husband and wife pleasure through sexual relationship within the bond of matrimony. (Hebrews 13:4)

Sexual relationship between a man and woman is out of the will of God if they are not married to one another. When God created Adam and took Eve from his side He gave His approval and that included their sexuality. "And God saw everything that he had made, and behold, it was very good. And the evening and the morning were the sixth day." (Genesis 1:26-31)

Satan is the one who perverted sexual relationships after he became god of this world system. (II Corinthians 4:4) Remember be honest with God and He will bring you out more than a conqueror. Saints there are issues we have to confront in our lives and with God's word we can become victorious Christians. Remember the same God that saved you can also keep you from falling if you want to be kept!

Chapter 2

Old Baggage

I John 1:6,7 says, "If we say that we have fellowship with him, and walk in darkness, we lie, and do not the truth: 7th But if we walk in the light as he is in the light, we have fellowship one with another, and the blood of Jesus Christ his Son cleanseth us from all sin." We are made the righteousness of God when we come to Christ and give our lives to Him, but we still carry the old baggage into our new life even though the blood of Jesus cleanseth us from all sin. Although we are saved we are yet being saved it's an on-going process. The letters "eth" in the word Cleanseth means a continuation not only was we forgiven of our past sin, but both present and future sins.

We don't practice sin, but if we sin we have an Advocate, with the Father, Jesus, Christ the righteous. (I John 2:1) Sometimes when babes come to Christ they hear Christians giving their fiery testimonies, and they want to pattern themselves after these Christians. It's true we overcome by the blood of the Lamb and the word of our testimony, but it would be nice if we could hear testimonies concerning other people struggles that they had and are having since they have been "Born- again." This is the purpose for this book to show you the things that I'm enduring, and the things I endured as a Christian.

Remember a testimony is a test that God has given you the answers to in His word. Sometimes "babes" need to hear we didn't pass every test, and we had to take some tests over until we got it right. Then young Christians won't feel like "Salvation" isn't for them or feel condemned because they didn't pass every test. Someone might say that's not faith, but faith is trust in God to bring us to the end of our struggles. We are yet learning "How to walk with God" and confession is good for the soul. Look at Abraham the "Father of Faith" he failed his tests more than once, but God worked with him until he could believe Him by faith. For example God had to get his wife, Sarah, out of a jam that her husband had put her in when he told her to say she was his sister. (Genesis 12:11-13)

What about Hagar, Sarah's handmaid, an innocent by-stander whom both Abraham and Sarah subjected her and their son, Ishmael, through painful trials because of their lack of faith? They failed their tests, but God continued to forgive and work with them until both Abraham and Sarah became the "Father" and "Mother" of many nations. (Genesis 17:5,15-16; Hebrews 11:11)

Then the scriptures said "Abraham believed God and it was counted unto him for righteousness." (Romans 4:3) There were weights (baggage) that both Abraham and Sarah had because of sin, but God use them to bring the promise seed, Jesus, into the earth in whom Isaac was just a type. Genesis 12:1-3; Galatians 3:16) Hebrew 12:1 says, "Wherefore seeing we also are compassed about with so great a cloud of witnesses, let us lay aside every weight, and the sin which doth so easily beset us, and let us run with patience the race that is set before us."

The Hebrew word "tsuwr"(beset) here means: to cramp, to harass, confine. The Greek word "euperistatos" (beset) means entangling, obstructing. This is in a hostile sense. The Spirit of God through Paul, the Apostle, told us in Galatians 5:1 "Stand fast therefore in the liberty wherewith Christ hath made us free, and be not entangled again with the yoke of bondage."

If the weights (baggage) had drop off completely when we gave our hearts to Christ, the Spirit of God wouldn't inspired the writer of the book of Hebrews to tell the body of Christ to lay aside every weight and the sin that doth so easily beset us. (Hebrews 12:1) Have you ever heard the saying, "Don't clean the fish before you catch it?" This little cliché means you haven't caught the fish yet so stop trying to shape and mold it (clean it). This is a true statement to many in the church its God's job to shape and mold new Christians not the church. In salvation people are always trying to tell baby Christians what they can and can't do mostly what they can't do in their Christian walk before they ever get rooted and grounded in the Lord. Look back at my testimony chapter "Abide in your Calling." See where the person tried to clean the fish by trying to do the job that was for the Holy Ghost alone, and caused a marriage to dissolve.

Sometimes we expect baby Christians to be perfect and we are not perfect. I know, because when my son gave his heart to Christ I would always ask him did he read his Bible today? Until one day God rebuked me, and said you can't be his Holy Ghost. From that day forward I was careful what I said to him, and I knew I had to grow in that area for I was a babe in the Lord too!

Jesus rebuked the religious leaders of that day with doing the same thing. Jesus said in Matthew 23:15 "Woe unto you, scribes and Pharisees, hypocrites! For ye compass sea and land to make one proselyte, and when he is made, ye make him twofold more the child of hell than yourselves."

We must allow God to shape and mold others in His own image. For we all have weights (baggage) that we brought into Salvation and some we picked up along the way. Paul began to write to the Philippians (Church) and began to confess his weaknesses, and then his strengths in Christ.

Philippians 3:12-13 says, "Not as though I had already attained, either were already perfect: but I follow after, if that I may apprehend that for which also I am apprehended of Christ Jesus. 13 Brethren, I count not myself to have apprehended: but this one thing I do, forgetting those things which are behind, and reaching forth unto those things which are before, 14 I press toward the mark for the prize of the high calling of God in Christ Jesus."

Chapter 3

New Creatures

"Forasmuch then as Christ hath suffered in the flesh, arm yourselves likewise with the same mind: for he that hath suffered in the flesh hath ceased from sin." (I Peter 4:1) When you have ceased from sin (stop sinning) you will go through "Withdrawal Symptoms." Withdrawal means a detachment from sin, whether emotional or physically and even spiritually; or a termination of the administration of a habit forming substance. It also means the physiological re-adjustment that takes place upon such discontinuation. The word "Withdraw" means to remove oneself from activity or a social or emotional environment.

Sam, an alcoholic, and Bob, a drug addict, went to their doctors for a checkup and both received a bad report. Their doctors informed them if they continue to drink and take drugs it would eventually kill them. Their doctors gave them the information to get the treatment that they needed. The treatments would cause them to live a productive life, and add years to their lives. This was a decision that they had to make if they wanted to live. This statement became an eye opening experience for both Sam and Bob and they began to see clearly. Reality began to set in for the first time in their lives. They consider carefully what their doctor had said, and both men decided that they wanted to live.

Every one of us at some point in our life will have to face reality the same way Sam and Bob did and make our own choice. Whatever our weakness or sin we must acknowledge them and realize "Jesus" is the answer. Like Sam and Bob in my example we had to make a decision when the Spirit of God began to draw us to Christ whether we wanted to live or die. (St. John 6:44) The Spirit of God showed us the wrong path, we were taking "the path of death," and if we continued on this path destruction was inevitable.   We could accept Christ Jesus or reject him we all have that choice.   Contrary to popular beliefs (false doctrine) we all will not be saved because Jesus died for mankind.   This is an individual thing all must accept God's gift, Jesus, as their personal Savior and Lord.   (John 3:16) "I call heaven and earth to record this day against you that I have set before you, life and death, blessings or cursing: therefore choose life, that both thou and thy seed may live." (Deuteronomy 30:19)

Paul, the Apostle, by the Spirit of God told the "Church" "something they have to do."   He says, "Stand Fast" "in the liberty" "wherewith Christ hath made us free", and "be not entangled again with the yoke of bondage." (Galatians 5:1)   I put the words in this scripture in quotes so you could see it's up to you.
Let's get down to the nitty-gritty and ask some questions: Why is the devil having God's people all over the newspaper and media boasting about another "Pastor" that he has caused to resigned from their ministry that God has called them unto because of infidelity?   Why is Satan causing saints to constantly bring "Christ" to an open shame because of their raggedy lives that they are living?   Then we shake our heads and began to judge that Pastor or that saint until it hits home and now we want to pray!

We began to feel the symptoms of sin and we began to obey it and the lust thereof.   Remember the word "feel" it is a very important.   "For therein is the righteousness of God revealed from faith to faith: as it is written, the just shall live by faith.   (Romans 1:17)   We don't live by our feelings, but the just shall live by faith.   We are "New Creatures" in Christ or a "New Creation."   II Corinthians 5:17 says, "Therefore if any man be in Christ, he is a new creature: old things are passed away; behold, all things are become new." Thirty-four years ago, June nineteen seventy-eight, I accepted Christ as my personal Savior.   From the first day until this day I was no more of a "New Creature" than I am thirty-four years later.

The difference from that time and now is I have grown in the grace and knowledge of my Savior and Lord, Christ Jesus. (I Peter 1:2) Even though we are "New Creatures" there is still "Something we have to do."

One of my Bible teachers in Bible College made a statement that shocked me. What she said was "Salvation is not the overall cure all." I thought that's a strange thing to say, but as I continue to listen to her then I understood what she meant by that statement. When "Salvation" comes into our lives it doesn't mean we are exempt from all our problems in fact they have just begun. Since we accepted Christ we still have problems, but now we have someone to fight our battles and His name is "Jesus." " And he said, Hearken ye, all, Judah, and ye inhabitants of Jerusalem, and thou king Jehoshaphat, Thus saith the Lord unto you, Be not afraid nor dismayed by reason of this great multitude; for the battle is not yours, but God's." (II Chronicles 20:15)

When Elohim brought His people out of Egypt with a mighty hand and a stretch out arm He began to give Moses laws and ordinance for them to live by. Exodus is the Old Testament book of "Redemption," and Leviticus is the book that teaches us how to walk and live a holy life before God. (Hebrews 12:14) "Follow peace with all men, and holiness without which no man shall see the Lord." Now that we have been redeemed from the curse of the law we must learn how to walk with God. While we have a lot of books in the "New Testament" that teaches concerning redemption through the blood of Christ, Jesus, the book of Hebrews and the book of Romans will teach us how to walk with Him. The whole Bible will teach you how to walk with Elohim we just have to study it for ourselves.   (II Timothy 2:15)

Christians, we must study our road map which is the "Bible." God has done everything He is going to do through His Son, Christ Jesus. II Peter 1:5 says, "And beside this, giving all diligence, add to your faith virtue; and to virtue knowledge. In fact read II Peter 1:5-7 verses they show us in detail--"Something we have to do."

Chapter 4

Facing Temptations & Conflicts

(Testimony)

Praise God I had been saved maybe eight or more years and God was doing great things in my life.   I had been called to the ministry in nineteen eighty-three as a Missionary and in nineteen eighty-four I was elevated to Missionary-Teacher.   I was preaching on the streets and in the church and God had open doors for me to go into other churches and preach the Gospel.   I even trained other ministers to preach on the streets and God was saving souls and blessing others.
Then I notice I started feeling things in my emotions that I really didn't want to experience.   So I went to the church and prayed everyday thinking this temptation is going away because I'm going to pray it away.   I began to confess that I was a New Creature old things have passed away behold all things has become new.   (II Corinthians 5:17)
Preachers, teachers, and saints whatever your position that God has called you in the body of Christ; we can preach, witness to souls, but there is coming a time of testing.   We will have conflicts that war within, and without that comes from the soul.   (Romans 7:23; James 4:1)
Our mind (soul) has to be renewed by the word of God. The Spirit of God will lead the natural man or the "Soul" will lead him whichever one we choose to yield our members too. (Romans 6:13)   In my book "Yielding Your Will Totally to God" I began to write we are made in the image of God.   We have a "Spirit", "Soul," and the "Body" houses both Spirit and Soul.   (Thessalonians 5:23)   The Spirit makes us God conscious, the Soul makes us self-conscious, and the body makes us world conscious.   In our daily walk we have to be led by the Spirit of God so we want fulfill the lust of the flesh. Read the seven and eight chapters of Romans and let God

enlighten the eyes of your understanding.

Getting back to my testimony one day after seeking Him daily one day as I came home from church praying about my temptations and conflicts I turned on the radio and God sent me the answer.   Pastor, Ronald Brown, was talking about the soul and God began to deal with me about studying the "Spirit," "Soul," and "Body" which I call the "Triune Man."

My body began to go through withdrawal symptoms and I was going through in my emotions through the soul (which is the seat of the emotions), and it was making my physical body do gymnastics because the natural man didn't want to die.   No I wasn't yielding to the symptoms, but we were going through the conflict because we decided to cease from sin. An alcoholic or drug addict that decides to come clean will go through withdrawal symptoms in their bodies and mind. They will experience sweating, shaking, and even seeing things that are not there.

Christian, our bodies and mind will go through withdrawal symptoms.   You will feel all kinds of things in your flesh (soul) and your old desires will try to get you to submit to them.   The body will experiences all types of lustful desires, but saints its' not your body it's in the mind (soul).   Good news we don't live by our feelings or what we see, but the just shall live by faith.   (Romans 1:17)   When we talk about feelings we immediately think of sexual sins, but it could be anger, drugs, alcohol, and fear to name a few.   Whatever, the hang-ups Jesus, was hung up for our hang-ups.   Now all you Pharisees, Scribes and, Hypocrites out there who say you never went through any temptations or got angry with anyone you know what the Lord called them.   He said, "Woe unto you, scribes and Pharisees, hypocrites!   For ye are like unto whited sepulchers, which indeed appear beautiful outward, but are within full of dead men's bones, and of all uncleanness."   (Matthew 23:27)

We will have "Withdrawal Symptoms" as long as we live in this earthly body.   Symptoms are just the indication or characteristics of a condition.   It's not really anything wrong, but it's a warning sign that lets us know that danger is ahead so we can exercise our spiritual senses. Do not ignore warning signs they are there to keep you from falling out of the grace of God. Don't think you are strong within yourself because the latter part of Zechariah 4:6 says, "Not by might, nor by power, but by my spirit, saith the LORD of hosts." My soul and body enjoyed having sexual relationship with my husband and all of a sudden the flesh wasn't receiving any gratification now that it was accustomed too for many years. So it started going through withdrawal symptoms; emotionally, (soul), and physically (body).

This is why Paul, the Apostle, says, in the Romans 12:1,2 "I beseech you therefore, brethren, by the mercies of God, that ye present your bodies a living sacrifice, holy, acceptable unto God, which is your reasonable service. 2 And be not conformed to this world: but be ye transformed by the renewing of your mind, that ye may prove what is that good, and acceptable, and perfect, will of God." Then I heard my Pastor, Apostle Crosby, say in a message I preached "Knowing the tactics of the enemy." When we have done all-we need to, "Stand", "Resist" and "Believe." Whichever one comes first in my case I needed to "Resist", "Believe," God, and "Stand." God gave me the victory and I passed the test, and I understood that the appetites and desires of the flesh couldn't make me yield to its' passions. I had and have a choice in this life to walk in the Spirit or to walk to the dictates of the lust of the flesh. Christian, you must understand that the appetites and desires of the flesh can't make you yield to its' desires. Romans 8:1 says, "There is therefore now no condemnation to them which are in Christ Jesus, who walk not after the flesh, but after the Spirit." Believer or sinner I am not perfect but I'm striving for perfection and I want you to know God will keep what you commit unto him. (Phil.1: 6)

This book is not to condemn you: For God sent not his Son into the world to condemn the world; but that the world through him might be saved. (John 3:17)

There was a time when I was going through multiple tribulations so I went to the "Citadel" to pray (many years ago), and as I was crying before the Lord my temptation walked in the door, and he put his arms around me and began to comfort me. For all inquiring minds it wasn't my Pastor. A flood of emotions ran through my mind and I quickly excuse myself to go to the ladies room. I was dealing with a number of things at this time and I just didn't need another thing on my plate if you get what I mean. I had intended to return to the sanctuary, but I went home instead. Unlike Joseph I wasn't seduced I just was going through many things and I didn't trust myself. Remember we are not strong within ourselves, but strong in the Lord and in the power of His might. Temptation is not a sin- only when you yield to it, then it becomes sin. (James 1:13-15; I Cor.10: 13) If you have fallen into temptation you can confess your sin and the blood of Jesus will cleanse you from all unrighteousness. (I John 1:9)

Chapter 5

Flesh Lusteth against the Spirit

"For the flesh lusteth against the Spirit, and the Spirit against the flesh: and these are contrary the one to the other: so that ye cannot do the things that ye would.   18Th verse But if ye be led of the Spirit, ye are not under the law." (Galatians 5:17-18)
Lasciviousness is name among the works of the flesh in the book of Galatians.   I heard a minister on TV give his definition of "Lasciviousness", and his definition was "Lust" with no brakes.   Webster's dictionary defines "Lasciviousness" of characterized by lust: lewd.   2. Exciting sexual desires.   We are going to use the first definition for "Lasciviousness" lust with no brakes.   (GAL. 5:19)
I need to point out before I go any further that all desires and passions that you have are not sinful.   Elohim, has placed in the soul of man to worship and love Him.   He gave both men and women these desires and passions so if you are not married it's not wrong if you desire a mate.   In fact I can tell you that God is the one who put that desire in you.   We have to re-train our souls to bless the Lord as David, the King, and Prophet, of God said in the division of Psalms 103.
In fact he commanded his soul to bless the Lord.   "Bless the LORD, O my soul: and all that is within thee bless his holy name."

Timothy, the Apostle, wrote in the I Timothy 4:1 "Now the Spirit speaketh expressly, that in the latter times some shall depart from the faith, giving heed to seducing spirits, and doctrines of devils.   Reader, read that whole fourth chapter of first Timothy, and you will understand it's important for the "Body of Christ" to keep on the whole armour of God.   (EPH. 6:11)
Satan is turning up the heat on the body of Christ for he knows he has but a short time.   (REV. 12: 12)

This book is written of some of my experiences that I have endured up to this point, but I want you to know Satan comes in season. He will be back and we must always prepare ourselves by hiding the word of God in our hearts that we might not sin against God. (Psalm 119:11)

Let's go back to one of the works of the flesh "Lasciviousness." Many times we think we can control our own desires and appetites of the flesh, but the truth of the matter is we must constantly depend on the Spirit of God. Solomon asked "Can a man take fire in his bosom, and his clothes not be burned?" The man that had seven hundred wives, princesses, and three hundred concubines understood how one could burn in his lust and never satisfy the desires and the appetites of the flesh. The word of God said Solomon's wives turned away his heart from God to follow after other gods. (I Kings 11:1-4; Proverbs 6:27) The Samaritan woman at the well had tried everything to satisfy her soul even after being married five times she realized nothing could satisfy her soul until she met Jesus. The Samaritan woman testified to the men of that city that she had met a man who told her everything ever she did. (John 4:1-29) Isn't that just like Jesus when He delivers us He will send us back to confront what use to be an issue or weakness in our life?

Jesus says, in John 7:37,38 " In the last day, that great day of the feast, Jesus stood and cried saying, If any man thirst, let him come to me, and drink. 37 He that believeth on me as the scripture hath said, out of his belly shall flow rivers of living water." Jesus told her to call her husband and come-hither. The woman said I have no husband. Jesus said unto her, Thou hast well said, I have no husband. For thou hast had five husbands; and he whom thou now hast is not thy husband; in that saidst thou truly. (St John 4:16-18)

Saint, and sinner before Jesus can do anything for us we must come clean. The Samaritan woman came clean when she said, "I have no husband." (John 4:13-14; 7:37-38) If the Samaritan woman received that living water and testified she never thirst again why are we, Christians, still thirsting after accepted him as our Savior?   Many come to Jesus, but they don't want to give up the desires and appetites of the flesh.   Jesus said that men love darkness rather than light. (John 3:19)

Believer, as long as we are in this mortal body we will have conflict concerning these two natures: the old sinful nature and the new nature of Christ we received when we accepted Christ.   If you don't allow the Spirit to control your desires you will find yourself walking after the lust of the flesh and you will eventually lose all control.   (Romans 8:1) Choosing to walk after the lust of the flesh will soon turn into "Lasciviousness," which means you don't have any control. If you continue to stir your emotions and others the leaven will turn into a lump, and get out of control!   You will found that you have open an avenue to the enemy, and now you can't control it, because it's no longer you its' the enemy.

Derek Prince wrote this in his book "God is a Match Maker": Don't indulge in flirtations or superficial relationships with the opposite sex.   It may seem exciting to stir someone's emotions and allow your own to be stirred, but one day you may discover that your emotions have gotten out of control.   Like the sorcerer's apprentice, who discovered the formula to release the water in a flood, but did not know the formula to recall it, you may discover you have released emotions you are not able to recall.

The result is an emotional entanglement with a person who is no way suited to be your mate.   Even worst we may get entangled with someone else's mate.   "Keep thy heart with all diligence; for out of it comes the issues of life."   (Proverbs 4:23)   Paul, the Apostle, says, "Stand fast therefore in the liberty wherewith Christ hath made us free and be not entangled again with the yoke of bondage." (Galatians 5:1) Saints, God has given to us His Spirit and the Spirit of God gives us the power to live according to His word.

"A new heart also will I give you, and a new spirit will I put within you: and I will take away the stony heart out of your flesh, and I will give you an heart of flesh.   27 And I will put my spirit within you, and cause you to walk in my statues, and ye shall keep my judgments, and do them." (Ezekiel 36:26,27)   I started reading the New Testament after I got saved thirty- four years ago to learn about Jesus, my Savior, and then I began to wonder "Could I live as a Christian?"   I came to my Father (God) in prayer and I began to ask Him how was I going to walk like the Bible instructed me to walk?   He softly told me He would never ask me to do anything that He hadn't given me the power to do. Don't misunderstand me I haven't arrived nor have I reached perfection, but Christ, Jesus is not only my Savior, but He is "Lord" of my life.

I'm striving for perfection every day, and He has brought me from a mighty long way.   I was so excited when God gave me that revelation that I didn't have to rely on my own strength, and the Spirit of God would give me the power to obey His word.   Reader you can be a "Victorious Christian" in every area of your life because of the power of the "Holy Ghost."   (John 14:18)

"I will not leave you comfortless: I will come to you." Jesus, began to tell his disciples that He had to go back to His Father, but He would give them another "Comforter."   (St. John 14-16 chapters)   The Holy Ghost, He, is our Comforter, and He will give us the power to walk and keep God's ordinances and statues.   (Ezekiel 36:26,27)   We don't have to depend upon our own strength, because we have the "Comforter" which is another name for the "Holy Ghost" dwelling inside of us!

Chapter 6

Sanctify Them through Thy Truth

Knowing the hour had come for Him to go back to His Father; Jesus prayed for His disciples, and all those followers who would believe on Him through their word. (St. John 17:1,17-20) Jesus prayed, "Sanctify them through thy truth: thy word is truth." (St. John 17:17) The word "Sanctification" means to set apart. Christians, will always be set apart through His word as long as we are in the earth. Paul, the Apostle, wrote to the Corinthian Church: "Wherefore come out from among them, and be ye separate, saith the Lord, and touch not the unclean thing; and I will receive you. 18 And will be a Father unto you, and ye shall be my sons and daughters, saith the Lord Almighty." (II Corinthians 6:17-18) Jesus prayed to the father that he wouldn't take the Christians out of the world, but that He would keep them from the evil.

We are not of this world even as Christ is not of this world. "And for their sakes I sanctify myself, that they also might be sanctified through the truth." (St. John 17:16-19) Christians, are the light of the world, and the salt of the earth; we must not hide our light under a bushel or let the salt lose its' savor. (Matthew 5:13-15)

Since we are the salt of the earth that is to give flavor to this world, and as salt preserves we are to resist the moral decay and corruption that is in society by living godly lives.

This is true, but why are so many Pastors standing up in their pulpit and announcing to their congregation that God has given them the permission to leave their wives and has allowed them to marry another? Many have walked and fulfilled the lust of the flesh and lost their first love. God is not going to allow a liar to tarry in His sight. Pastors, God will hold you responsible for leading his people astray!

We understand there are circumstances where a mate doesn't

want to be reconciled to their husband or wife, and you can't make someone love you, but to leave your mate, because you are tired of them is not of God!

Saved men and women stop thinking because your husband or wife is a Christian you can abuse them and withhold your bodies from them, because they are saved. They were men and women before they became Christians or leaders. Many think their wives or husbands have to stay with them no matter how they treat them, because they are Christians and prominent leaders in the ministry. "Hog Wash!" Marriage is not the overall cure all either there are conditions that God put in His word for us to abide by in our marriage. A word to the wise is sufficient. (II Timothy 2:19) "Nevertheless the foundation of God standeth sure, having this seal, The Lord knoweth them that are his. And Let everyone that nameth the name of Christ depart from iniquity."

Why are so many Christians committing fornication and adultery? Hebrews 13:4 "Marriage is honourable in all, and the bed undefiled, but whore-mongers and adulterers God will judge." Christians there are many works of the flesh, but adultery and fornication is the sin that sinneth against the body.

(I Corinthians 6:18-20) "Flee fornication." Every sin that a man doeth is without the body, but he that committeth fornication sinneth against his own body. 19 What? know you not that your body is the temple of the Holy Ghost which is in you, which ye have of God, and ye are not your own? 20 For ye are bought with a price: therefore glorify God in your body, and in your spirit, which are God's."

We, the body of Christ, have gotten off course and have begun to travel on the wide road that leads to destruction for we say the majority rules. Believer, God has more than seven thousand in the body of Christ who hasn't bowed down to "Satan." We must repent and do our first works over again! Paul had to write the Corinthian Church because they believed that sex was as necessary as food was for the body. I Corinthians 6:13 says, "Meats for the belly, and the belly for meats: but God shall destroy both it and them.

Now the body is not for fornication, but for the Lord; and the Lord for the body."

Paul, the Apostle, wrote the Corinthian Church in II Corinthians 11:2 "For I am jealous over you with godly jealousy: for I have espoused you to one husband, that I may present you as a chaste virgin to Christ." Christ, Jesus is coming back for a Church without a spot or wrinkle or any such thing. We are not male dogs that when we get in heat go and search for a female dog, or female dogs waiting and standing until a male dog comes to us. This is their nature, but we, are human beings, who are made in the image of God and after His likeness. He has ordained "Marriage" between "Male" and "Female." Even God gave animals the instinct to know they are to breed together with the opposite kind of their animal counterpart. (Genesis 8:17) This is for all those who believe they are born "Homosexuals and Lesbians."

We are not writing this book to condemn anyone for Jesus came not to condemn the world, but that the world through him might be saved. (St. John 3:17) Elohim loves us and He is listening with his ear waiting to hear our voice of repentance. He told Ezekiel to warn both the wicked and the righteous man for it gives Him no pleasure in the death of the wicked, but that the wicked would turn from his wicked ways and ye live. (Ezekiel 18:32) Elohim (God) is not waiting for us (Christians) to make a mistake or sin so He can destroy us for He loved us so much He gave His only begotten Son.

We must continue to have a repentance spirit and confess our sins daily. (I John 1:9-10; 2:1-2) "But if we walk in the light, as he is in the light, we have fellowship one with another, and the blood of Jesus Christ his Son cleanseth us from all sin. 8 If we say that we have no sinned, we deceive ourselves, and the truth is not in us." (I John 1:7,8) Jesus' blood even after we have accepted Him as our Savior and Lord continues to cleanse us from all sin.

When we confess our sin Elohim forgives us so forgive

yourself, and don't allow Satan to condemn you. Even as I'm writing this book Elohim is showing me my shortcomings, and I'm laying aside every weight and the sin that doth so easily beset me. (Hebrews 12:1) When we look into the word of God we are beholding our natural face in a glass and like Isaiah we cry "Woe is me" For I am undone; because I am a man of unclean lips, and I dwell in the midst of a people of unclean lips" for my eyes have seen the King, the LORD of hosts." (Isaiah 6:5)

Remember, God uses ordinary people and we are not perfect, but we are striving for perfection. God told Ezekiel to eat the whole roll himself and not to be like that rebellious house. (Ezekiel 2:8) "But thou, son of man, hear what I say unto thee; Be not thou rebellious like that rebellious house: open thy mouth, and eat that I give thee." Leaders, and saints from the pulpit to the door we are not exempt from obeying God's word for the sword of the spirit (word of God) is a two-edged sword. (Hebrews 4:12; Psalms 119:11)

Chapter 7

Be Transformed

Romans 12:2 "And be not conformed to this world: but be ye transformed by the renewing of your mind, that ye may prove what is that good, and acceptable, an perfect will of God."

In twenty-nine years of my walk with Christ as a single woman I learned how to do the work of an "Evangelist." When I was married I was a wife and a mother and I was learning about the Lord. When I became a single woman I devoted my time to the Lord and trained my son in the way he should go. I began to witness and preach in the streets in Jerusalem, (my neighborhood) that kept me busy for the Lord. Then I launched out into the deep to other neighborhoods, and cities, (Judaea-Samaria) then God blessed me to preach in "Frankfurt Germany" (uttermost part of the world). (Acts 1:8)

Elohim, blessed me for my faithfulness through my son and his wife by sending for me to visited them in "Frankfurt Germany." I began to witness in his building and souls came to Christ. Many great things happened in Frankfurt Germany, and one of the many blessings God bestowed on me was meeting Pastors Eddie and Cassandra Thornton, and their Church family. I'm sharing with you this part of my life to show the body of Christ that if we keep busy doing the work of an "Evangelist", and the "Ministry of Reconciliation" we want have time to think about "Self." James says, every man is tempted, when he is drawn away of his own lust and enticed. (James 1:13-15)

When I began do the work of an "Evangelist," going out witnessing and praying for others it kept my mind on the Lord. I wasn't meditating on being a single woman anymore, or what I was going through in my body, and focusing on my trials. When I took care of "God Business"

He took care of mine. Saints, you have to live life where you are until God gets you to the place where you are going. "Therefore take no thought, saying, What shall we eat? or, What shall we drink? or, Wherewithal shall we be clothed?" (Matthew 6:31) "But Seek ye first the kingdom of God, and his righteousness; and all these things shall be added unto you." (Matthew 6:33)

Paul, the Apostle, prays for the Church of Thessalonians: "And the very God of peace sanctify you wholly; and I pray God your whole spirit and soul and body be preserved blameless unto the coming of our Lord Jesus Christ." We are spiritual beings made in the image of God and after His likeness. (Genesis 1:26; I Thessalonians 5:23) Adam, still had the Spirit of God in him even after sin enter the earth when he disobey God, but now God no longer quicken (make- alive) His Spirit in him. (Gen. 2:16-17; Eph. 2:1) Elohim didn't quickened Adam's spirit or anyone because "Sin" had entered the earth, and the sin debt had to be paid. The wages of sin is death, but the gift of God is eternal life. Adam couldn't pay the price for man's sin, because through him all men have sin. (Romans 3:23; 5:12; 6:23) Sin has to be dealt with and Elohim killed an animal and shed its' blood for their sin. They were both spiritually naked before God so He clothe them in righteousness with the blood of an innocent animal. Then they wore coats of skins on their bodies. Elohim, used the blood of animals as a sacrifice to pay the price for their sin temporarily until Christ, Jesus came through 42 generations and die once and for all. (Matthew 1 chap; Hebrews 11:28)

When sin entered the world men began to operate through their "Soul" nature that made them "Self Conscious." (Genesis 6:5; Romans 5:12) When Adam yielded to the Spirit, of God, the Spirit controlled the "Soul" and the "Body" before he made the choice to disobey God. I'll put it this way the body will follow the Spirit or the Soul and this is the choice each Christian has to make for their own life. If we allow the Spirit to be in control of our lives we will live in victory, but if we obey the dictates of the soul we will live in defeat.   (Romans 6 chapter)

When Adam disobeyed God sin came in and he died, and now he is dead in his trespasses and sin. (Genesis 2:16-17; Ephesians 2:1) When a sinner hears the word of God and repents and is converted then God quickens His Spirit within him and he becomes a new creature. (John 5:21; 6:63; Romans 10:14-15; I Corinthians 5:17) Believer, as long as we are on this earth God will quicken His Spirit in our mortal bodies as we continue to seek after Him. (Romans 8:11) "But if the Spirit of him that raised up Jesus from the dead dwell in you, he that raised up Christ from the dead shall also quicken your mortal bodies by his Spirit that dwelleth in you." If it took the word of God to quicken us and the Spirit to draw us to Christ when we were dead in our trespasses and sins, it will take the same word to keep us saved. (Eph 2:1: Rom. 8:11)

An important word to the sinner and backslider: God's Spirit will not always strive with man. (Genesis 6:3) Giving you an example in the first chapter of this book I gave my testimony about how Satan destroyed my marriage- go back, and read that chapter. My husband kept calling me and asking me to go back with him, but I didn't respond and one day he stopped calling. One day God will stop quickening His Spirit in us if we keep rejecting His word, and then it will be too late. Sinner and backslider don't let this happen to you heed the call of God as he is quickening His Spirit in you as you hear His word. (Romans 10:14-17)

We must stop thinking about "Self" and start thinking about "Eternity." Where will your immortal soul spend eternity in Heaven or Hell? When the believer begin to think about "Self" we are drawn away from God because of lust and when it is conceived, it bringeth forth sin and when it is finished, sin bringeth forth death. (James 1:15) Even though Adam and Eve were spiritual beings they had a Soul and a Body. When Adam and Eve began to think that God was withholding something from them they began to think about "Self." This is how we get in trouble in our flesh because we start thinking about "Self."

Stop looking at "Self" and look unto Jesus the "Author and Finisher" of your faith. Transformation comes when we renewed our mind through the word of God. We must continue to read God's word to renew our minds and this must become a way of life for every believer. (Romans 12:2) Our bodies need nutrition and the vitamins that from food to live everyday unless we are fasting and praying. So does the Spirit and Soul need spiritual food that comes from the word of God. When Satan tempted Jesus to turn the stones into bread Jesus said it is written: "Man shall not live by bread only, but by every word that proceedeth out of the mouth of God doth man live." (Deuteronomy 8:3; Matthew 4:4) Notice Jesus didn't say man doesn't need bread for his "Body." Man needs both Spiritual and Natural food for he is a Spiritual being, and he has a Soul and he lives in a Body. His Body houses both his Spirit and Soul. (I Thessalonians 5:23)

Christians, learned how to be content in whatsoever state that you are in believing God to bring you up, out, and above the storms of life. Paul, the Apostle, began to write to the Philippians Church: "Not that I speak in respect of want: for I have learned, in whatsoever state I am, therewith to be content." (Phil. 4:11) Paul, the Apostle, testified that he knew how to be abased, and he knew how to abound, and this is a place where we all must strive to enter as born-again Christians. (Phil. 4:10-12)

Chapter 8

Deception

Now the Spirit speaketh expressly, that in the latter times some shall depart from the faith, giving heed to seducing spirits and doctrine of devils.   (I Timothy 4:1)

Webster's dictionary defines "Seduce"- to lead (a person) away from duty or proper conduct; corrupt 2.   To induce to have sexual intercourse. 3. A. To entice or beguile into a desired state or position. B. To win over; attract. Lust 1. Intense or unrestrained sexual craving. 2. An overwhelming desire or craving: a lust for power. I wanted to give you different meaning of the word seduce which comes from the word "Seduction."

Elohim (God) had given Adam, the representative, of the human race instructions how to walk with Him in complete harmony. In Genesis 2:16,17 verses He told Adam of the provisions that he had made for him, and then he gave him a simple test. He instructed him not to eat of the "Tree of Knowledge of good and evil" and explained the consequences if he disobeyed.

Reader read my first book "Yielding Your Will Totally to God" where I explained the first earth that Lucifer ruled, and the recreated earth that Adam had dominion over before he committed high treason to obey Satan instead of God. Satan's planned was to take the third part of the angels and go to the third heaven and usurp authority over his Creator and set on the throne of God, but his plan failed.   (Isaiah 14:12-14; Ezekiel 28:11-16; Jeremiah 4:23-26; Genesis 1:2) Satan lost his first estate (position) with Elohim (God), because of rebellion.   Elohim shook the inhabitants that Satan ruled off the earth and recreated the second earth, and gave it unto Adam to rule. (Isaiah 24:1) Satan has lost his position over the first earth, because of rebellion and now his goal is to seduce Eve through one of his power twins called seduction.   (Genesis 1:2; I Peter 3 Chapter)

Satan's plan is to seduce Eve to influence Adam, the representative, of the earth to rebel against God, his Creator, by getting him to eat the forbidden fruit. The purpose is to get Adam to give his dominion and authority over the earth to him willingly. (I Timothy 2:13-14) Remember reader, God has a plan for your life and Satan does too! "For I know the thoughts that I think toward you, saith the Lord, thoughts of peace, and not of evil, to give you an expected end." (Jeremiah 29:11)   Satan's plan is to steal, kill, and destroyed our souls, but Jesus came that we might have life and that more abundantly. (John 10:10)

Saints, Satan, is an alien, in the earth, and he has no dominion or authority over you. He has to use the spirit of deception to manipulate the Christian into giving his authority over to him willingly. (I Tim. 2:13-14) Let's see how Satan used his power twins "Seduction" and "Lust" to deceive Eve. Always remember the person who is the seducer has been seduced himself. "Seduction and Lust" are the power twins of Satan working together to divide God and His Son, Adam. (Luke 3:38)

Satan comes to divide and conquer. His goal is to take the recreated earth from Adam and rule in his place. (II Corinthians 4:4)   Eve, was the bait, that Satan used to lure his prime target, Adam, by one of his power twins called seduction. When we read the third chapter of Genesis it seemed like Satan just seduced Eve overnight, but he didn't because seduction takes time it's a process. (Genesis 3:1-6) Remember reader, I said the word "Seduce" in this case means to lead (a person) away from duty or proper conduct.

Satan, watched Eve, and studied her, as scientist studies the behavior pattern of different species of animals. His strategy was to isolate her from her husband, and get her alone with him so he could seduce her.   That's the first thing Satan does to God's Sheep (people) he isolates them from their Shepherd (God) and their Pastor. Then he isolates them from other spiritual-minded Christians so he can deceive them (us). He listened to her conversation with her husband and he watch her even when she was alone.

What Satan noticed about Eve is that she had three gifts: the gift of gab, curiosity, and the gift of influence, because at some point she moved toward the direction of that tree. Satan used the serpent to deceive her because of her curiosity, and use her to influence her husband to eat the fruit of the tree of knowledge of good and evil. I believe he studied both Adam and Eve his opponents like a fighter studies his opponents in a previous fight that was taped before he enters the ring. Many fighters do this to locate their opponents strengths and weakness. Satan's goal was to steal, kill, and destroy and cause Adam to give him his dominion and authority over this world system. Even though sin had not entered the earth Adam, and Eve were created free mortal agents. They had the power of choice to obey or disobey God, their, Creator. I believe Adam and Eve enjoyed their relationship with God, their Creator, and each other a long time before they disobeyed God.

Satan comes out of his corner of the ring like a boxer anticipating the victory over his enemies. He comes to steal, kill, and destroy with his spiritual weapons, "Seduction & Lust." He focuses on Eve because he wasn't confident that he could seduce Adam. Listen, men Satan doesn't want you to know that he is afraid of you because you are the "Representative" of your home and you have the vision for the "Church." This is why Satan doesn't want you to know the position that God has placed you in the body of Christ. Satan wants the men to stand on the outside looking in never assuming their position that God has given them in the "Home" or the "Church." A word to the women before I continue the plan of Satan's attack against Eve, his bait he wants to use our gifts: the gift of curiosity and influence the wrong way. These gifts used properly can bless our husbands. We must gird up the loins of our minds so that we can be the help meet God called us to be by reading His word. The wives of the home and the women of the church birth the vision in the home and the Church. Women we can't let Satan use us to destroy our men.

We must put on the whole armor of God, and having done all we must stand. (Ephesians 6:13) We must stand on God's word that Satan doesn't only fear our husbands or our sons, but that he will fear us also, because of the word of God in us that dwells in us richly. Satan was really after Adam, but he believed he had a better chance to use his wife, Eve, to get to him. I must explain why Satan was after Adam and not Eve. Adam was the representative, of the human race, and he had dominion and authority over everything in the earth. In other words "Adam" was the god of this world. (II Corinthians 4:4)

This is my theory Eve could have eaten every fruit that was on the "Tree of Knowledge of Good and Evil" and nothing would have changed. There was no poison in the fruit of the "Tree of Knowledge of Good and Evil" it was used for the sole purpose to test Adam. Satan knew that Adam was the one he needed to seduce to eat the fruit in order to cause him to disobey God's word. Then he would gain the dominion and authority over the recreated earth, and become god of this world system. (II Corinthians 4:4) Satan is an alien, that had no legal rights or power in the recreated earth so he had to deceived Adam, the "Representative," of the "Earth" into giving his power over to him. To have power in the earth you have to be born here.

That's why the "Word" (Jesus) had to be born in the earth through a virgin. Isaiah 7:14 says, "Therefore the Lord Himself shall give you a sign; Behold, a virgin shall conceive, and bear a son, and shall call his name Immanuel." (Luke 1:27-35) John 1:14 says, "And the word was made flesh, and dwelt among us, (and we beheld his glory, the glory as of the only begotten of the Father,) full of grace and truth." God, the Word, had to come through a virgin Himself made in the image of God so he could become the "Representative" of the Earth to redeemed man back to Himself. (Galatians 4:4,5) Oh the wisdom of God! Let's go back to Adam and Eve and recognize the plan of Satan to steal, kill, and destroy Adam and Eve. (John 10:10) Eve's, curiosity concerning the "Tree of Knowledge of Good and Evil" was Satan's chance to seduce her. He watched her and planned his strategy a long time before he zoomed in for the kill. In Genesis the second chapter the latter part of the ninth verse says, the Tree of Life was also in the midst of the garden and the Tree of Knowledge of Good and Evil. (Genesis 2:9)

Both of the trees were in the midst of the garden, but Eve kept looking and moving toward the "Tree of Knowledge of Good and Evil." Seduction is a powerful weapon of Satan because it lures its victims like a spider lures its' prey into the spider web. The flesh always wants something that it can't have. Remember this took place before the fall, and Paul, the Apostle, said there is no good thing that lies in the flesh. This is how "Lust" works together with Seduction because "Lust" is the weapon that craves, and it wants the power to be in control of every situation. Only God, is Sovereign, and is in control of every situation. The seducing spirit kept drawing Eve to the "Tree of Knowledge of Good and Evil" over a period of time. Finally Adam and Eve both were standing at the "Tree of knowledge of Good and Evil" listening to Satan lies. Jesus said concerning Satan in (John 8:44) "Ye are of your father the devil, and the lusts of your father ye will do. He was a murderer from the beginning and abode not in the truth, because there is no truth in him. When he speaketh a lie, he speaketh of his own: for he is a liar, and the father of it."

It might have taken years for Satan to seduce Eve and get both of them over to the "Tree of Knowledge of Good and Evil" because the word of God never said Eve called or went to get Adam. "Seduction" lured Adam and Eve to the Tree of Knowledge of Good and Evil, and "Lust" was the second spiritual weapon Satan used in his strategy to convince both Adam and Eve that God was withholding something from them.

Saints, when we start thinking about "Self" that's when we get in trouble. Satan's first strategy was to bring doubt on God's word so he used her second gift, the gift of gab, to talk with the serpent. (Genesis 3:1) "Now the serpent was more subtile than any beast of the field which the LORD God had made.   And he said unto the woman, Yea, hath God said, Ye shall not eat of every tree of the garden?"   Now that Satan has Eve's attention he began to talk to her through the serpent about the Tree of Knowledge of Good and Evil. Seduction gets your attention and lust causes you to crave both the desire and the power.   Now that Satan has their attention he's still isn't confident concerning Adam, because he, hasn't said anything.   Satan is not a mind reader he can only attack us through our words of doubt and unbelief. (Prov.18:21)

Eve began to give the serpent an explanation about the trees in the midst of the garden.   She told Satan they could eat of the trees, but of the fruit of the tree that was in the midst of the garden they couldn't eat or touch it lest they die. (KJV-Genesis 3:2-3)   Saints we don't owe Satan an explanation just put him where he belongs under your feet. Two trees were in the midst of the garden: The Tree of Life, and the Tree of Knowledge of Good and Evil.   Elohim never spoke anything about the Tree of life.   He told them they could eat of every tree of the garden except the Tree of Knowledge of Good and Evil.   He never said they couldn't touch the trees this is a good example of a person adding to the word of God.   (Genesis 2:16-17)
Satan's plan was working he had her attention and he moved in for the kill with Lust his spiritual weapon.   Genesis 3:4 says, "And the serpent (Satan) said unto the woman, Ye shall not surely die."   He brought doubt on God's word by telling them they wouldn't die.   Satan knew he had her attention and he began to work like an old professional flimflammer, and before they knew what hit them they had eaten the forbidden fruit.

Satan told them God knew that if they ate of this tree their eyes would be opened and they would be as gods, knowing good and evil.   Satan appealed to the woman with his spiritual weapons of Lust: The Lust of the Flesh, Lust of the Eyes, and Pride of life.   (I John 2:16; Genesis 3:6) "When the woman saw that the tree was good for food, (lust of the flesh) and that it was pleasant to the eyes (lust of the eyes), and a tree to make one wise, (pride of life) she took of the fruit thereof, and did eat, and gave also unto her husband with her; and he did eat. Now Satan had set his sights on getting the dominion and authority from Adam and becoming the god of this world system.

Adam, who was the representative, of the Human race had dominion an authority over every creature in the earth he just stood there and let Satan steal, kill, and destroy his home. He willingly gave his dominion and authority over to Satan by disobeying the word of God. (I Timothy 2:13-14) It doesn't matter whether Adam knew about Satan, his archenemy, or not because God gave him the dominion over every creature and the serpent is a creature. We understand that Satan used the serpent, and all Adam had to do was to use his dominion and authority over this creature and cast him out of the garden and the earth. I made this statement earlier in my text, but I believe it needs to be repeated until we can get the understanding of their position.

They had the power and authority over the serpent (Satan), but neither Adam nor Eve used their authority. If they had used their authority over the serpent--Satan, would have lost the victory, and couldn't have gained access into the recreated earth. Satan was here illegally and the only power he had was the power that both Adam and Eve gave him. We (Christians) give our power to Satan every time we disobey God's word. To have dominion and authority in this "Earth" you must be born here or you can steal it from someone who was created from the "Earth" like Satan did Adam. He stole the dominion and authority from Adam through deception. Now Satan is the god of this world system. (II Corinthians 4:4) "In whom "the god of this world" hath blinded the minds of them which believe not, lest the light of the glorious gospel of Christ, who is the image of God, should shine unto them." Take courage reader, I believe God in his infinite wisdom gave Adam a lease over the "Earth" to have dominion and authority for six- thousand years. In Revelation 12:12 it says, "Therefore rejoice, ye heavens, and ye that dwell in them. Woe to the inhabiters of the earth and of the sea! For the devil is come down unto you, having great wrath, because he knoweth that he hath but a short time." Satan's lease of the "Earth" and his dominion and authority as the god of this world system is coming to a close.

His lease will not be renewed, because God never leased it to Satan--He leased it to Adam. Meanwhile Jesus, the Last Adam, came and took the dominion and authority back from Satan that Adam gave him through his disobedience. (Romans 5:12,17-18) Jesus, legally defeated Satan because He was the "Word of God" manifested in the flesh. (St. John 1:14) He gained everything that Adam had lost through his death and resurrection. He has redeemed us from the curse of the law. (Galatians 3:13) Reader, we must understand that even as Jesus gained the dominion and authority of this "Earth" back from Satan we must accept Christ as our Savior and Lord in order to gain the victory over Satan. Pause at this time reader, and ask God (Elohim) to forgive you of your sins.

Chapter 9

Confronting Issues

(Godly Nature & the Sinful Nature)

The word "Confront" means to come face to face with, esp. with defiance or hostility. Saints don't be afraid to confront issues in your life. "Ye are of God, little children, and have overcome them: because greater is he that is in you, than he that is in the world." (I John 4:4) The woman with the issue of blood didn't have any rights according to the Law of Moses being in the midst of the crowd nor could she touch anyone in her condition because whatever she touched would become unclean. (Leviticus 15:19-21) She had suffered many things of many physicians, and spent all that she had and was nothing better and grew worse. (Mark 5:25-34) The woman with the issue of blood had been isolated from her family, and friends for twelve long years, but when she heard that Jesus was coming it renewed her faith. She went against the grain and everything that she was taught and knew she could have been stoned for disobeying the Law of Moses. I believe she spoke the same words to herself as the four leprous men did; "Why sit we here until we die." She became a desperate woman who decided I'm going to confront this issue and press my way into the crowd and touch the hem of Jesus' garment and be healed of this issue of blood.

The word of God said when she touched the hem of Jesus garment the fountain of blood dried up and she was healed of that plague. I say earlier one of my Bible, College teachers, made this statement; "Salvation is not the overall cure all." I believe that statement meant it doesn't mean we are exempt from problems because we have given our hearts (lives) to Christ, Jesus in fact I can assure you that your problems has just begun.

Cheer up believer because the difference between being a sinner and becoming a child of God is having God on our side. He fights our battles and gives us the victory. Reader the day you gave your heart to Christ, Jesus, I know it seemed like all hell broke loose, and it probably did because Satan is mad for he has lost his foot hold that he had in your life.

Read the book of "Exodus" and see how God instructed Moses to go down to Egypt and tell Pharaoh (type of Satan) to let his people go and as soon as Pharaoh heard this he made their task harder. (Exodus 5:Chapter) Satan will throw his darts at us when we give our lives to Jesus and try to entangle us again with the yoke of bondage. (Galatians 5:1) He doesn't want to give up ownership, but there isn't anything he can do about it if we continue on in the Lord. We don't belong to him because we have been bought with a price and we are no longer our own. Satan isn't the owner of our soul anymore if we have accepted Christ as our Savior and Lord. We may say "Satan" wasn't my owner, but John 8:44 says, "Ye are of your father the devil, and the lusts of your father ye will do. He was a murderer from the beginning, and abode not in the truth, because there is no truth in him. When he speaketh a lie, he speaketh of his own: for he is a liar, and the father of it." Paul, the Apostle, was inspired to write by the Holy Ghost: (Galatians 5:1) "Stand fast therefore in the liberty wherewith Christ hath made us free, and be not entangled again with the yoke of bondage."

When we become Christians we don't know what to do when our marriage is threatening a divorce or we find out that our children are on drugs, and many other trials that we face in this life. Saints I admonish you don't allow your trials to move you from your faith in God. We must determine we shall not be moved, but be like a tree that's planted by the rivers of living water. (Psalms 1:3) Go into His word and see "What does the word say?" When I was eight years old my father took me to the doctor because he realized something was wrong. When he would talk to me I didn't answer, and I could tell this frustrated him, because he thought I was ignoring him or daydreaming.

The truth of the matter was I didn't hear him talking to me, because I was having a seizure. It seemed like I was daydreaming and I would snap out of it and say what did you say or I didn't hear you? I didn't bite my tongue or shake violently when they first started at the age of eight.

The doctor told my father that I was having a seizure. It started off with what seemed like daydreaming and he told Him I would never be healed. He also instructed him if I got married to tell my husband to be that I had seizures. I was a child and when I heard the bad news that I would never be healed I was devastated. The doctor was talking to my father as if I wasn't in the room, and besides this I was only eight years old. During this stage in my life this was an issue. I had just heard the doctor say I would never be healed or there was no healing for this condition. Praise be to God, that was the doctor's diagnosis (word), but God's word says, (I Peter 2:24) "Who his own self bare our sins in his own body on the tree, that we, being dead to sins, should live unto righteousness: by whose stripes ye were healed." Then as I grew older I began to have "Grand mal seizures." I had them for twenty-two years, but then my spiritual father, Dr. Apostle A. J. Jackson, introduced me to Jesus. I gave my heart to Jesus, and begin hearing the word of God and studying His word for myself especially the scriptures on healing. Faith comes by hearing and hearing by the word of God. (Roman 10:17)

Satan didn't want to let me go, but I didn't let him move me from my faith in God's word even when He tried to attack me with the symptoms. I stood my ground. I continue to confess the word of God that I was healed by His (Jesus) stripes. Reader, some was healed as they went to show themselves to the Priest and some were healed miraculous, but all was healed! (Luke17: 11-19) Satan may tell you that you call yourself a Christian and what are all your Christians friends going to think when they find out your marriage is threatening a divorce or the doctor diagnosed you with cancer etc.   He will get you to thinking about your self-image and how you need to play a role and act like everything is all right.   We are ashamed because we confess Christ and it seems like this shouldn't be happening to us!

 I was going through in my body as I confessed that I would walk in divine health and by Jesus' stripes I was healed.   (I Peter 2:24).

        I stood up boldly in church and everywhere I went I was boldly professing this confession-"By Jesus stripes I were healed."   Remember we overcome by the blood of the Lamb and by the word of our testimony.   (Revelation 12:11) Satan thought he would stop me dead in my tracks and gave me a seizure (symptom) in church.   He thought that would stop me!   It just gave me a push to confess what God's word said about my healing.   I stood my ground and continue to testify by Jesus' stripes I were healed.   Some saints didn't understand and looked at me funny and whispered behind my back and said I thought Sister Barbara said she was healed. I didn't take it personally, because they weren't the only ones who didn't understand.   I didn't understand either, but I knew I wasn't allowing Satan to move me from my faith in God.   God didn't ask us to understand what we are going through He asked us to believe His report (word). Understanding will come later as it did for Joseph (Genesis 45:7,8), but we must endure our hardships as a good soldier of Jesus Christ.   (Isaiah 53:1; Romans 10:16; II Timothy 2:3) Reader God's word is true and it didn't matter whether I had a seizure or not God's word is forever settled in Heaven. (Psalm119: 89)

        The seizure that I had didn't make the word of God of none effect.   God's word is true anyhow!   I didn't understand all that was going on in my life, but I wasn't going to allow Satan to make me doubt God's word.   I confess sometimes that I was worrying, and other times I just went through this period in my life.   God turned it around for good for he has given me the Gift of healing and working of miracles.   Not only those gifts, but also other gifts and He have called me to teach His word!   I know His word works because I have worked the word. We are not omniscient like God, but we must trust him with our lives! I admonish everyone to read your Bible along with this book. You would be amazed at the lives of the people that God called and made "Covenants" with and how they had horrible things to transpire in their lives. If God can change them in their time greater things will He do in us because we have a "Better Covenant" established upon better promises! God began to tell me to read about the different "Covenant Men" and their families, and as I began to read all I can say is what a mess.

Jacob stole Esau his brother's birthright, because he was a sup planter (deceiver) and Esau gave his birthright away for a bowl of porridge. Joseph brothers wanted to murder him, but God intervened, and they decided to sell him for twenty pieces of silver to the Midianites for a price of a slave. (Genesis 37-50 chapters) These were "Covenant Men" people who represented the God of Israel. So don't get discourage because you are a Christian and all hell seems to break loose in your home remember "God is in Control." There were other families who were "Covenant Men" with God who went through difficult times, but God brought their families out more than a conqueror!

Hebrews 12:2 says, "Looking unto Jesus the author and finisher of our faith; who for the joy that was set before him endured the cross, despising the shame, and is set down at the right hand of the throne of God. Do you know what the word "despising" in this verse means? It means to discount or to deduct or subtract from a cost or price. Jesus didn't discount the shame He endured for mankind. That was part of the price He paid as He allowed them to do all the horrible things they did to Him. It was for us so we could lift our heads up when we go through! Remember Christians if you live godly you will suffer persecutions.

When I began to read the word of God it began to give me hope that He was changing me every day into the image of His dear Son. He is changing you if you trust in his word and allow Him too. (II Corinthians 3:18) Lift up your heads O ye gates and let the King of Glory come in. Who is the "King of Glory" the LORD strong and mighty! (Ps. 24:7) I understand that we are not exempt from problems, and trials that we experience in this life as you will, but remember God is in control. The world, (sinners), hides from their problems by medicating their pain through drugs, alcohol, and many other things that trick the mind. These things don't solve anything it just makes matters worse. Some born-again, Christians, live in a fantasy world, and won't confront issues in their lives, and believe God is going to do everything for them. Paul, the Apostle, tells us what to do in Romans twelfth chapter first and second verses.

We need to pray and confront those issues we encounter in the church and in this life with the word of God. We can't be like the Ostrich that sticks his head in the sand and thinks its hiding because its' body is seem by all. Our issues are not going away and we must confront them with prayer and, the word of God.

When we confront the issues in our lives with the word of God we will become "Victorious Christians." I heard my former Pastor, Apostle Jackson, said "If you don't deal with the deal it will deal with you. We must face every issue that comes up in our life, and like David we must pray and ask God "Shall we Pursue?" (I Samuel 30 Chapter) We must face reality and ask God to help us to know the difference between reality and living in a fantasy world. Jesus came to die and He rose again so we want have to live in a fantasy world. Many Christians may not drink or take drugs anymore, but they medicate their pain by living in a fantasy world. Faith is not living in a fantasy world it is trusting in God's word, and not in our circumstances. Take a moment and ask yourself "What does the word say about my circumstance?" If it's healing you need go into the word of God and seek God's word on the subject of healing. Here are just a few scriptures on healing (Isaiah 53:1-5; I Peter 2:24) Don't be a lazy Christian seek God and ye will find Him.

Let's get back to the series of test that we all must go through even our Lord and Savior was tested. (Matthew 4 Chapter) To all the "Religious Pharisees" and "Self-

Righteous Scribes out there I'm not addressing you because you have your own place that God is going to send you unless you repent quickly. Shake off that religious spirit and know that we (Christians) will be tested in three ways: "Lust of the flesh, Lust of the eyes, and Pride of Life. (I John 2:16)

Praise God I realized as a saint and as an Elder in my church I haven't arrived. I told you I was one of the "Elders" in our Church because sometimes we think because of the calling upon our lives we have arrived. We must hear God say these precious words "His lord said unto him, "Well done, thou good and faithful servant: thou hast been faithful over a few things, I will make thee ruler over many things: enter thou into the joy of thy lord." (Matthew 24:21) Listen God is not impressed with our ministry gifts He is the one who gave them to us, but he is impressed when we live holy and righteous in our homes, on our jobs, schools, and everywhere we go. He wants us to let our light shine.

Saints if God has planted you in a church and given you leaders after His own heart- pray and support them with your finances and your time. I admonish leaders, sub-leaders, and saints everywhere from the pulpit to the door that as long as we are in this body we will always have trouble in the flesh. We will always go through tests, but the Gospel is good news. God has given us the answers to every test in His word, and has given us the power of the Holy Ghost to bring us out more than a conqueror! I heard a "Man of God" say we are perfect, I totally agree, but we are not perfect in our flesh. We, (Christians,) who are born-gain our spirits are perfect, but our soul and body has not been born-again. Paul, the Apostle, writes to the Roman Church that there are two things we must do with our bodies and our mind (Soul). Romans 12:1,2, says, "I beseech you therefore, brethren, by the mercies of God, that you present your bodies a living sacrifice, holy, acceptable unto God, which is your reasonable service. 2 verse And be not conformed to this world: but be ye transformed by the renewing of your mind, that ye may prove what is that good and acceptable, and perfect, will of God."

Our bodies and soul will be redeemed, but they haven't been redeemed yet that's why Paul, the Apostle, was inspired by the Holy Ghost to write to the Roman Church instructing them what to do with their bodies and their minds (Soul). Romans 8:23 says, "And not only they, but ourselves also, which have the first-fruits of Spirit, even ourselves groan within ourselves, waiting for the adoption, to wit, the redemption of our body."   Reader read Romans the sixth chapter through the eighth chapters and if you want to be blessed read the entire book of Romans.   We have both a godly nature and a sinful nature and we must choose which one we will obey.   (Romans 6:16)   Galatians 5:17 says, "For the flesh lusteth against the Spirit, and the Spirit against the flesh: and these are contrary the one to the other: so that ye cannot do the things that ye would.   18th verse But if ye be led of the Spirit, ye are not under the law."   Then in that same chapter Paul, the Apostle, began to list the works of the flesh. Paul, the Apostle, recognized the serious problem he was having in the flesh (carnal-mind) after his conversion. His sinful nature was overtaking his godly nature because he was a babe and was learning how to walk with God!   He confessed in Romans 7:15 "For that which I do I allow not: for what I would, that do I not; but what I hate, that do I. Paul, the Apostle, goes on to say in the sixteenth and seventeenth verses "If then I do that which I would not, I consent unto the law that it is good.   17th v "Now then it is no more I that do it, but sin that dwelleth in me."   Paul, the Apostle, began to cry out in Romans 7:24-25 - "O wretched man that I am!   Who shall deliver me from the body of this death?   25th verse I thank God through Jesus Christ our Lord.   So then with the mind I myself serve the law of God; but with the flesh the law of sin.   Then in the eight chapter of Romans Paul, the Apostle, writes to the Romans Church and to body of Christ- Romans 8:1 "There is therefore now no condemnation to them which are in Christ Jesus, who walk not after the flesh, but after the Spirit."

Paul, the Apostle, is talking about the two natures that dwells in every believer the godly nature and sinful nature. He through the Holy Ghost tells us how to become an over-comer. He tells us if we walk not after the flesh (what we feel through our Soul-emotions), but after the Spirit we will not fulfilled the lust of the flesh. Walking after the Spirit means to obey God's word and not walking in what our five senses (emotions) dictates to the body. We must let the Spirit of God in us be in control of our bodies and emotions (Soul). For we walk by faith, and not by sight. (II Corinthians 5:7) David, the Prophet wrote in Psalms 119:11 "Thy word have I hid in mine heart, that I might not sin against thee." We must hide the word of God in our heart from the pulpit to the door. Saints years ago thought only their leaders and other ministers had to know the word of God and some think that way today. We must change our way of thinking and arm ourselves likewise with the mind of Christ. (I Peter 4: 1) Christ Jesus is coming back for a church without a spot or wrinkle or any such thing. (Ephesians 5:27) We, the Body, must gird up the loins of our minds and confront the issues in our own life like the woman with the issue of blood did and went to Jesus the only one who could deliver her. Leaders, sub-leaders, don't let the devil deceive you whatever the test you are going through. Run to Jesus and realize none of us is exempt from tests I don't care how God uses you! Christ Jesus' blood not only cleanses us from sin it continues too! Salvation is a process and we are always learning about our Father, God, and His Son, Christ Jesus, through His word and by the teaching of the Holy Ghost. My heart and prayers goes out toward leaders because they are on the front line and they help so many souls, and it seems like we, saints, don't even want to pray for our leaders. I don't care how God is using them they need our prayers, finance, and time. Concerning the issue of "Money" if we want to come out of debt and be blessed we are going to have to stop mumbling and complaining about giving our natural things (money) to support the "Men and Women of God" especially our Pastors. I Corinthians 9:11- "If we have sown unto you spiritual

things, is it a great thing if we shall reap your carnal things?"
Leaders have preached the Gospel and minister to us by the
laying their hands on us, and deposited many spiritual gifts in
our lives and much more.   We should be glad to give unto
them our natural (finance) things.   We can't beat God
giving.   If we sow seed God is going to multiply the seed
sown.

Chapter 10

Behave Yourself Wisely

I will behave myself wisely in a perfect way. O God when wilt thou come unto me? I will walk within my house with a perfect heart." (Psalm 101:2)
 David was considered a reject amongst his own family. Even his father didn't consider him kingship material after all he was just a Shepherd boy. Why didn't Jesse send for David when the Prophet, Samuel, said to him gather all your sons together to the sacrifice that I might anoint one to be King of Israel? Wasn't David a son of Jesse? (I Samuel 16:5,11) Shepherds were considered a low class of people. Paul, the Apostle, wrote "But God hath chosen the foolish things of the world to confound the wise; and God hath chosen the weak things of the world to confound the things which are mighty." (I Corinthians 1:27)

David had a relationship with God, the Shepherd, of his soul, and he wasn't concerned what people thought about him because he knew God loved him. God chose David from amongst all his seven brothers to be King over Israel, but when he became king, he committed adultery, and had Bathsheba's husband killed. How soon David forgot what the Lord had done for him, and how He had taken him up out of the miry clay and had established his goings. (Psalm 40:2)

Now the judgment of God has passed upon his family, and nothing seemed to be going right. Like a driver on a slippery icy road that swirls from side to side, and loses all control of his car David, realized his life was out of control. Now that he was king he made wrong choices and these choices destroyed his relationship with God and his family.

He must go back and regain his relationship he had with God when he was just a Shepherd boy. He abused the authority and power that God had given him as the King of Israel. Elohim got David's attention when He allowed all the tragedy to come upon his family and kingdom because of his rebellion against Him. I preached a message from David's life, and the topic was "It costs too much to sin." (Romans 6:23) Take time and read that true story about David and Bathsheba and you (we) will realize the importance of behaving yourselves wisely. (II Samuel 11 &12 Chapters)

We must let God build character in our life through the "Fruit of the Spirit." Temperance means self-control and it is one of the seeds of the fruit of the Spirit. Temperance and the other seven seeds of the "Fruit of the Spirit" that Paul, the Apostle, wrote about comes from "Love" the main fruit. "Agape" (Love) comes directly from the Spirit of God. (Galatians 5:22-23) The Preacher (Solomon) wrote, "Love is strong as death." (Song of Solomon 8:6)

He also said "Many waters cannot quench love neither can the floods drown it." Don't be a lazy Christian search out the rest of these scriptures. I admonish you to read your Bible daily and then read good Christian books. What has God put in your hand or charge lately? Have you lost control like King David? He commits adultery, kills Uriah, Bathsheba's husband, and if God hadn't intervened and fixed the brakes in his life he would have lost all control. That's what the word "Lasciviousness" means "Lust" with no brakes. If your answer is yes you (we) need "Temperance." The power of God can fix your brakes and give you back control of your life.

When we are born-again the Spirit of God brings the "Nine Fruits" of the Spirit into our human spirit.. (Galatians 5:22) Let's go back to the seed of the fruit of the Spirit call "Temperance" which means tempered or self-control. We don't have to ask for the Fruit of the Spirit because the Holy Ghost brings them into our human spirit once we give our hearts to Christ. Our job is to yield to them and let them have the right away in our lives. Temperance helps us have "Self Control" over our circumstances and over all things that we may face in this life.   We all need "Self Control" because we have two natures the godly nature that we received when we accepted Christ, Jesus as our Savior, and LORD, and the sinful nature that dwells in us because of the first Adam.   (Romans 5:12-19)   Through Adam's, disobedience all were made sinners and have a sinful nature, and through the last, Adam, (Jesus,) many are made righteous and have a godly nature. (I Corinthians 15:45) "For the flesh lusteth against the Spirit, and the Spirit against the flesh: and these are contrary the one to the other: so that ye cannot do the things that ye would." (Galatians 5:17)

This is why we need to walk in the Spirit and not fulfill the lust of the flesh. We are the ones who must decide who will have the preeminence in our lives the lust of the flesh or the Spirit of God.   David committed many sins in his lifetime, but it is written of him that he was a man after God's own heart.   (Acts 13:22) "And when he had removed him, (King Saul) he raised up unto them David to be their king; to whom also he gave testimony, and said, I have found David, the son of Jesse, a man after mine own heart, which shall fulfill all my will."   When I first read the life of David I didn't understand how God could say that David was a man after His own heart until I understood that God looks on the heart not on the outward appearance.   (I Samuel 16:7) "But the Lord said unto Samuel, Look not on his countenance or on the height of his stature; because I have refused him: for the LORD seeth not as man seeth: for man looketh on the outward appearance, but the LORD looketh on the heart." We have to confess like David "I will behave myself wisely." We must not confess with our mouth only, but our actions should come from the heart (soul) because it is an act of our "Will."   Read my first book "Yielding your Will Totally to God."   I said earlier God is not impressed with our preaching, singing, and prophesying He wants us to behave ourselves wisely in the home; on our jobs, in our churches, and everywhere we go.   Remember we are representing God! Stop saying that's just how I am, and allow God to make and mold you.   (II Corinthians 3:18) "But ye all, with open face beholding as in a glass the glory of the Lord, are changed into the same image from glory to glory, even as by the spirit of the Lord."

Christians and sinners I ask you to give God a chance in your life so he can change you into the image of His dear Son. This takes time so don't just quit the first time you sin repent, and God will forgive you and then rise up and out of your stupor, and forgive yourself. (I John 1:9; 2:1)   Remember saints God doesn't condemn us that is the tactic of the devil. If I had to wear a sign on me it would say: "Please be patience with me God is not through with me yet."   I'm yet growing every day into the image of his dear Son, Christ, Jesus.   We all know what our weaknesses are no one has to tell us because the Holy Ghost has already revealed it to us.   Some get angry at the drop of a hat, some have no self-control when it comes to the opposite sex, and some are liars. Don't worry if I haven't named any of your sins you know what they are, but let's be honest with God and ourselves so He can help us. Satan has been studying us a long time turn the pages back to the eight chapter of this book, and read how Satan studied both Adam and Eve before he seduced them.   Let's flip the script and studied our archenemy, Satan, and tear his kingdom down.

Chapter 11

The Lover of My Soul

Do you like to read romance books? Did you know the Bible is a romance book from God to all people? Elohim is my "Husband," and we have been married thirty years. I celebrated our anniversary in the month of June 08 because I was united in a "Covenant" relationship with Him since June 1978. In thirty years He has given me the power through the Holy Ghost to be true to Him! He has fulfilled and is fulfilling all my needs according to His riches in glory. (Philippians 4:19) He has loved me when I came up short and He has loved me when I made Him proud. Elohim (God) told me I could always come to Him about everything that concerned me in my walk with Him, and He would in no wise cast me out. Have you ever been ashamed of the different temptations that you wanted to yield too because of the things that you felt in the flesh? Maybe you wanted to slap someone who put you down or you just wanted to throw in the towel.

Pastors, have you said, "What the use?", and thought about leaving your pulpit and never pasturing or ministering to another soul. Maybe someone who is reading this book has yielded to that temptation. Many times when we think about temptations we think about sexual enticement or sexual sin. Leaving your pulpit as a Pastor or slapping someone who put you down are real issues that saints face every day. Paul, the Apostle, wrote to the Galatians, and Christians today concerning the works of the flesh that we should be Spiritual minded not walking after the flesh, but being led by the Spirit. (Galatians 5:19-21) Paul, the Apostle, says, "If we live in the Spirit, let us also walk in the Spirit."

Cheer up if you have yielded to the temptation don't despair Elohim is a loving and forgiving Husband. Elohim began to woo me to Him for He knew that I wasn't proud of myself because of the things I felt in my flesh. I was still a babe and I didn't realize that temptation is not a sin only when you yield to the temptation. I came to my Husband, (God), and I began to cry out to Him and tell Him how I felt. He began to whisper sweet things in my ear by His Spirit, and tell me I never have to be afraid of anything that I was dealing with, and to continue to be honest with Him in prayer. I could come boldly to the "Throne of Grace" to obtain mercy and to find grace to help me in the time of need. (Hebrews 4:16) He told me you are in the flesh, and the flesh might feel anything, but I didn't have to yield to what I felt.

He said He made me a woman and He made me to desire a man. Paul, the Apostle, wrote in the I Corinthians 10:13- "There hath no temptation taken you but such as is common to man: but God is faithful, who will not suffer you to be tempted above that ye are able; but will with the temptation also make a way to escape, that ye may be able to bear it." I realize that if I delight myself in Him He (God) would give me the desires of my heart. (Psalms 37:4) God has a plan for my life and I have given everything to him because He is the Lover of my Soul. I submitted myself to Him for He is the Author and Finisher of my Faith. (Hebrews 12:2)

There are different temptations that I was tempted in the flesh to do, but God always gave me the strength in my weakness that made me an over-comer. (St. John 16:33) Did we pass every test? No, but we studied the word of God so we wouldn't have to take that test again.

Romans 1:17 says, "For therein is the righteousness of God revealed from faith to faith: as it is written, The just shall live by faith." Reader, if you have yielded to temptation Elohim's love for you will never change, but you must repent. Please remember when you asked God to forgive you that He has forgiven you, and cleanse you from all sin. (I John 1:9)

Take it a step farther and forgive yourself and don't allow the enemy of your soul to condemn you.

The book of the "Songs of Solomon" hasn't been taught that much in the church, and I don't call myself an expert on this particular book, but I know someone who is the teacher of the word of God and He is the "Holy Ghost." In this chapter "The Lover of my Soul" I will use the book of the "Songs of Solomon" to show you how much Elohim (God) loves us and the lengths and depths He will go to win over our love that He may give us the riches of His love. Many people think they are rich because of the possessions they have accumulated in this life, but like the Church, of Laodicea, Jesus had to rebuke them.

Revelations 3:17, 18- "Because thou sayest, I am rich, and increased with goods, and have need of nothing; and knowest not that thou art wretched, and miserable, and poor, and blind, and naked: 18th verse I counsel thee to buy of me gold tried in the fire, that thou mayest be rich; and white raiment, that thou mayest be clothed, and that the shame of thy nakedness do not appear; and anoint thine eyes with eye-salve, that thou mayest see."

The "Song of Solomon" can be interpreted many ways through the power of the Holy Ghost: "Love between Elohim (God) and His chosen people Israel, " "Love between Christ and the Church," "Love between Husband and Wife," and "Love between Solomon, and a rustic, Shulamite, girl." I want you to focus on God's love that He has for you through His Son, Christ Jesus. (Isaiah 54:5; II Corinthians 11:2; Ephesians 5:23-33; Songs of Solomon 1-8 Chapters) Reader, take out time to read those chapters.

Many can quote the Bible verse (St John 3:16) " For God so loved the world that He gave his only begotten Son, that whosoever believeth in him, should not perish, but have everlasting life." We, Christians, are guilty of doubting God's love although we have experienced His love when we first gave our hearts to Him. Trials and tribulations have made us lose our first love.

Never let the devil or anyone tell you He doesn't love you because of the things you are going through. Paul, the Apostle, asked us a question: "Who shall separate us from the love of Christ? Shall tribulation, or distress, or persecution, or famine, or nakedness, or peril, or sword?" (Romans 8:35-39). Jesus reminds us of his word when He said no man taketh my life, but I lay it down that I might take it again. This commandment I received of my Father. (St. John 10:17-18) Reader don't think God doesn't love you anymore because of the trials you are experiencing right now in your life. He can be touch with the feeling of our infirmities so come to Him and He will heal you. (Hebrews 4:15) Many have low self-esteem like this Shula mite girl even after responding to Solomon's love because of the hard taskmaster she was controlled by in the pass. (Songs of Solomon 1:5,6) Satan was a hard taskmaster, and we still feel the pain of the pass because of many issues that occurred in our life before Salvation. Go back to the ninth chapter and read it over again and allow God to give you the strength through His Son, Jesus Christ, to confront every issue in your life so it will become a thing of the pass. We heard in our lifetime that we would never amount to anything or our parents or someone else expected too much from us. We were always trying to get others to affirm their love for us.

Pastors, are hurting and feeling like giving up because their members are unfaithful and have lost their first love. Husband and Wives are disappointed because their spouses are not paying them any attention anymore and the romance (love) and passion has gone out of their marriage. Parents, are disappointed because their children didn't live up to their expectations, and finally children want to divorce their parents because they're not getting the attention they need. When we put confidence in any of these examples we are looking for love in all the wrong places. "Jesus is the Lover of our Soul."

The word of God says, Solomon had seven hundred wives, princesses, and three hundred concubines and his wives (strange women) turned away his heart. (I Kings

11:3). Even though Solomon had all these wives it is said that this rustic, "Shula mite girl," capture his heart and he fell in love with her. Solomon began to make advances or go after this rustic "Shula mite girl." Solomon was a powerful and rich man who had everything to offer her, but she remained faithful to the one whom she was to marry. It was said of the Shula mite girl that she was to marry a man who came from the same background and country where she lived, but God, the matchmaker, who's divine purpose and plan was the marriage union between this "Shula mite girl" and Solomon. When we began to read this book we find she has low self-esteem and many problems in her life. The Shula mite girl with all her problems still had no desire for Solomon in the beginning. Solomon continued to woo her to win her affections with his love until one day she responded to him, and he brought her into his palace. When we accepted Christ, Jesus, as our Savior, He brings us unto Himself and we are baptized into the body of Christ. We become heirs with God and joint heirs with Christ, and Heavens' best belong to us not only in this world, but the world to come. (Romans 6:3; 8:17; Galatians 3:27)

Solomon in the "Songs of Solomon" is a type of Christ, Jesus who draws us with His Spirit and loves us in-spite of how we continue to reject Him over and over even after we become Christians. Christ, Jesus loves man (you) His most prize creation above all the creatures, countless angels, the moon, and the stars that He created. (Colossians 1:13-16). Pondered this in your mind how Elohim (God) skipped over all other creatures and made (you) men in His image and in His likeness and He wants to have an intimate relationship with you (us). (Genesis 1:26)

That's why David, the Prophet, wrote Psalms 8:3-9- "When I consider thy heavens, the work of thy fingers, the moon and the stars, which thou hast ordained; 4TH verse What is man, that thou art mindful of him? And the son of man, that thou visitest him? 5th verse For thou hast made him a little lower than the angels, and hast crowned him with glory and honour.

That is how Solomon is a type of Christ, Jesus, he skipped over all his wives and concubines to win the love of this rustic "Shula mite girl."Like the Shulamite girl we had many lovers: the lust of the flesh, the lust of the eyes, and the pride of life.   We were in love with an alien, called "Satan," and we rather obey him and do his bidding than God, our Creator. He was a hard taskmaster, and he abused us, but we kept coming back for more because he promised us many riches.

Christ, Jesus, continued to draw us with His Spirit to bring us unto Himself.   (John 6:44) "No man can come to me, except the Father which hath sent me draw him: and I will raise him up at the last day."   The latter part of Jeremiah 31:3   says, Yea, I have loved thee with an everlasting love: therefore with loving-kindness have I drawn thee.   Yet we kept ignoring Him because what he had to offer us didn't appeal to us or seemed to be a beautiful and rich life. We looked on the outside of the Tabernacle of Christ and we just saw the ugliness of the Goat's hair, Ram skins, and the Badges skin that covered Him.   Isaiah 53:2)says, "For he shall grow up before him as a tender plant, and as a root out of a dry ground: he hath no form nor comeliness; and when we shall see him, there is no beauty that we should desire him."

Once the Shula mite girl responded to Solomon's love she still felt unworthy although she saw the riches of all the things she ever wanted once she came inside the palace. Once we surrender and accept Christ, Jesus as our Savior, and Lord and come inside the True Tabernacle into the "Holy of Holies" we began to see the beauty and riches of Christ, Jesus ,that He has to offer us not only in this world, but the world to come.   Christ, Jesus, is omnipotent, and only He can fill the void in our lives.   He gives us all riches to enjoy and that includes healing for the whole man.   (I Thessalonians 5:23; Galatians 3:13)   He said I've come that ye might have life and that more abundantly.   (John 10:10)

When the Shula mite girl finally responded to Solomon and was brought into his palace she carried the baggage of the abuse of this world that caused her to have low self-esteem. She began to tell the other virgins not to look upon her for she was black, but comely and she said her mother's children made her the keeper of the vineyards, but my own vineyard I have not kept. (Song of Solomon 1:6)

In the Song of Solomon, Solomon, assures her of his love for her. He calls her his dove and lets her know he is her protector and he is eager to enter into a relationship with her. "O my dove, that art in the clefts of the rock, in the secret places of the stairs, let me hear thy voice, and thy countenance is comely." (Songs of Solomon 2:14) Elohim (God) loves us so much He waits to hear our voice, and He protects, and provides for us for He is the "Good Shepherd."(Psalm 23)

Can you fathom in your mind Elohim, the God, of the Heavens and the Earth is eager to form an intimate relationship with you (us)? Little old me? That's what I said "Little old me?" Doesn't that just build your self-esteem to a higher level of faith in Him when we finally realized God wants to be our Father and we become His children? Yet many of us in the Body of Christ have lost our first love for we have become lukewarm Christians toward the lover of our Soul. Jesus said to the Church of Laodicea's I know thy works, that thou are neither cold nor hot, but lukewarm and because you are lukewarm I will spue thee out of my mouth." (Revelation 3:15-16)

King Solomon made his presence known to the Shula mite girl and came to fellowship with her, but she had already lain down for the night. She was comfortable and didn't want to get up, but when she finally decided to rise up out of her bed to open the door he was gone. (Songs of Solomon 5:2-6) We are like the Shula mite girl we want to fellowship with the Lord when it's convenient. It seems like Elohim comes in an inopportune time, but whenever God's presence fills our heart and He wants to fellowship with us it is always the right time day or night.

It doesn't matter whether we are going through a series of test or trials, or had just lain down for the night. God said His Spirit would not always strive with man. (Genesis 6:3)

We see Solomon seeking after the Shula mite girl and wooing her unto himself.   In the fifth chapter sixth verse it says, "I opened to my beloved; but my beloved had withdrawn himself, and was gone: my soul failed when he spake: I sought him; I called him, but he gave me no answer." (Songs of Solomon 5:6-8)

Sometimes God will withdraw Himself from us so we will seek after Him.   Saints of God He said He would never leave you nor forsake you, but remember this relationship is two--sided.   We see Solomon seeking after the Shula mite girl and wooing her unto himself.

The Shula mite girl finally learns to relax and seeks after the one who sought her in the pass.   (Songs of Solomon 5:6-8) Elohim (God) tells us to seek Him while He may be found, and call upon Him while He is near.   (Isaiah 55:6-7)   Christ Jesus is the "Lover of my Soul" and He wants to be yours also. He can love all of us, and not be unfaithful to anyone, and He proved His love for us for he laid his life down, and rose again the third day for our justification.   (Romans 4:25)   I invite you to come into the True Tabernacle for there are hidden riches to be found in Christ Jesus.

There is peace in the midst of turmoil, joy in the midst of sorrow, and love that's strong as death.   (Song of Solomon 8:6)   "Set me as a seal upon thine arm: for love is strong as death; jealousy is cruel as the grave: the coals thereof are coals of fire, which hath a most vehement flame."   Let Jesus become the "Lover of your Soul."

Chapter 12

To The Precious Men of God

"Thine Husband"

Men of God you may be asking the question "How can God be my Husband?

Let's look at Isaiah 54:5 in the King James Version it reads "For thy Maker is thine husband; the Lord of hosts is his name; and thy Redeemer the Holy One of Israel; the God of the whole earth shall he be called." Then Elohim goes on to say in the sixth verse "For the Lord hath called thee as a woman forsaken and grieved in spirit, and a wife of youth when thou wast refused, saith thy God."
Elohim's goal is to elevate our thought life to a higher level that He may reveal Himself to the inner man. (Isaiah 55:9-11). He is talking to His people, the nation of Israel, which consists of both men and women who are familiar with the intimate relationship between a husband and his wife. In the "Songs" you will witness God's love toward you and His people. He wants you to understand the depths and heights of His love that He has for all people.

He says He is their Maker and thine Husband. Let's look at the meaning of the word "Husband" in this verse of scripture.
"Husband" in the Hebrew Strong's Dictionary 1167 ba'al means Master, Husband, Lord, and Owner. So we see it's not just talking about "Husband" as we think of the word "Husband and Wife," but Husband as God being your Owner, Master, and Lord of your souls.

Men this will help you see Elohim in the right perspective as you begin to identify with Him as your "Husband." Since He is your Master, Owner, and Lord you can be all the man you can be and not be intimidated by the enemy. Elohim called Adam and made him the little god of this world, and gave him dominion over all things in the earth.   (Genesis 1:26-30)   Now through Christ, Jesus, the Last Adam, He has taken what Satan has stolen from Adam, and has given us dominion and authority that Adam had before he sinned.   (Romans 5:12; Colossians 2:15)

Men who have been rejected at some point in their life may find it difficult to love someone or themselves.   This is why Matthew the twenty-second chapter and thirty-seven through thirty-nine verses are very important scriptures. When we love God with everything that is in us we can love ourselves, and then we can love our neighbor.

David, a type of Christ, knew what it meant to be rejected.   His family rejected him not knowing he would be chosen to be the next King of Israel, but God prepared him by allowing David to go through with Saul, the first King, of Israel.   His life was in danger many times before he became king and he had to run from King Saul, and others even after his kingdom was established.

Elohim wanted to give an example of His love for men so that they could comprehend that the little "Eves" could not fill that void in their life.   God gives us an example of Him knitting Jonathan's soul with the soul of David. (I Samuel 18:1-3)   Two souls knitted together represented the marriage covenant.   When a man and woman consummate their marriage the two become one flesh.   Elohim wants men to comprehend He is thine Husband when they accepted Christ, as their Savior.   They have entered into a marriage covenant and are joined to Him and have become one Spirit.   (I Corinthians 6:15-17)   Jonathan, a type of Christ, a friend, who sticketh closer than any brother made a covenant with David, and stripped himself of his royal robe and gave it to David.   (Proverbs 18:24;I Samuel 18:4)   Jesus, who was the "Word," in the beginning came from heaven and stripped Himself of His royal robe, and made Himself of no reputation, but took upon Himself the form of a servant.   He made a Covenant with you (me) and sealed it with His blood.
(St. John 1-14; Phil 2:6,7; Heb.8-9 Chapters)
When David heard about Saul, the King, and his friend, Jonathan's, death he was distressed.   He began to say, "How

are the mighty fallen in the midst of the battle!   O Jonathan, thou wast slain in thine high places.   I am distressed for thee, my brother Jonathan: very pleasant hast thou been unto me: thy love to me was wonderful, passing the love of women." (II Samuel 1:25-26)

Elohim didn't want to leave Himself without a witness of His love for men.   He portrayed the love between two men for each other to show His love for men. This was a godly love between friends.   Jonathan and David's love portrayed Christ, Jesus' love for mankind.
Many have distorted this picture that Elohim portrayed concerning David and Jonathan's love for one another, and tried to insinuate that there was a homosexual relationship between them.   Satan wants us to believe this lie because he doesn't want men to know how much God loves them.
Elohim began to knit Jonathan's soul to David's soul   to show men the love of Christ, and the extent He will go to prove His love for them even the death of the cross.
Christ, Jesus, can be touched with the feeling our infirmities because he was tempted in all points as we are yet without sin. (KJV-Hebrews 4:15)   The word of God says, in the book of Isaiah that Christ Jesus was despised and rejected of men; a man of sorrows, and acquainted with grief: and we hid as it were our faces from Him and we esteemed Him not.   (Isaiah 53:3)

Jesus knows what it means to be rejected.   He knows how you feel so He is inviting you to lay your head on His breast, and witness the love He has for you. (John 13:25)   His love is greater than the Delilah's of this world try Him for yourself if you haven't accepted him as your Savior and Lord. Men in order to love your wife and others you must first love God.   You will not even know you are in the beloved except you love Him.   The first and greatest commandment: Thou shalt love the Lord thy God with all thy heart, and with all thy soul and with all thy mind (Matthew 22:37)

Chapter 13

Wrong Relationships

Did you know that sometimes God will allow us to feel what He feels? So He will take us through what seems like a difficult situation.
Let's look into the life of the Prophet, Hosea, and see how Elohim revealed to him how He felt about His people, Israel. God's people were unfaithful to Him and rejected His love and care for them no matter how He blessed them.
Elohim needed to relay a message to His people, Israel, so he instructed Hosea, the Prophet, to marry Gomer, the Harlot. (Hosea 1:2) Sometimes it seems like Elohim places us between a rock and a hard place, but He always has a reason for everything that He does. First, He wants to show us two things ourselves, and second, He wants to give us a greater revelation of Himself. I notice in my own walk with the Lord when I'm going through difficult situations this is the time when I can see my weaknesses and my strengths. You'll never know what your weakest and strongest areas are until you go through that trial. So cheer up if you going through a difficult situation right now because God might want to use you to relay a message to His people or someone close to you.
The infidelity of Hosea's wife, Gomer, helped the Prophet, Hosea, understand why God was grieved with His people who were worshipping idol gods whom He had redeemed. Hosea had married Gomer, a Harlot, and was faithful to her and cared for the children that she got outside their marriage. Hosea loved his wife, Gomer, and he was going through some painful heart breaking moments because of her unfaithfulness, and if that wasn't enough one night she didn't come home. I imagined he was worried and didn't know what had happen to her so he searched for her and found his wife being sold for a price of a slave on the slave market. Elohim instructed Hosea to buy her back who was an

adulteress. (Hosea 3:1)   He redeemed her back with fifteen pieces of silver, and a homer and a half homer of barley. (Hosea 3:2)   He was glad to purchase what already belong to him because he loved her.   That's what the word redeem means to buy back what already belongs to you.   Hosea, being a type of Christ, redeemed Gomer, his wife.   Jesus redeemed us back unto Himself because the first Adam sold us into the slavery of sin.

Now Hosea, can deliver God's message with an impact to His people, Israel, because he feels the pain and grief that God felt when his own wife was unfaithful to him.   Reader I want you to see another side to this true story of the Bible concerning Hosea and Gomer.   Did you ever wonder why Gomer wasn't satisfied with her husband that was faithful, and who   forgave her many times for her unfaithfulness?   Hosea, the Prophet, did everything for his wife, Gomer, and loved her with everything that was in him yet she still wasn't satisfied.   Ladies we know a good man is hard to find much less a God, fearing man, right?   The answer that Jesus gave the lawyer will give us insight into why Gomer wasn't satisfied with a "Man of God" who gave her everything.

Matthew, the Apostle, wrote in his gospel that both the Pharisees and Sadducees had join forces together to tempt Jesus after He had put the Sadducees to silence.   A lawyer asked Him -Which is the greatest commandment?   Jesus said unto him, "Thou shalt love the Lord thy God with all thy heart, and with all thy soul, and with all thy mind.   This is the first and great commandment. And the second is like unto it, Thou shalt love thy neighbor as thyself.   On these two commandments hang all the law and the prophets." (Matthew 22:37-40)   I type it so you could read it for yourself.   These scriptures are the keys to right relationships and they help us comprehend why Gomer didn't love her husband, Hosea. Wrong relationships manifest themselves in our lives when we don't take the time to fellowship with our heavenly Father. The word in Matthew twenty-second chapter thirty-seven to the forty verses gives us the formula to right relationships.

Our first priority is to love God with all our heart, soul, and might. Elohim kept His Covenant with His people yet they disobeyed His word.   Relationships are two-sided and both parties must work together in building a right relationship. Gomer, was a Harlot, and she didn't love the God of Israel with all her heart, soul and might.   She loved what she was doing because she did it over and over.

It didn't matter how her husband love and care for her, Gomer, couldn't receive his love because she didn't love herself.   Remember the order in Matthew 23:37-40.   The order is to love God first and then you can love yourself. Remember the second commandment, Thou shalt love thy neighbor as thyself. That's the key loving yourself then you can love your neighbor (others).   The Lord may give you a warning my sister or brother concerning the person you're about to marry.   Don't ignore the warning signs that are telling you to wait until they grow in that area of their life. I must warn both sinner and saint alike we can't love someone and think that's going to change them only Jesus can delivered them.   You may say within yourself if I love them and treat them like a King or Queen I can change them. We must work the formula, God's word, and then we can have right relationships.

Gomer, whose name meant "Completion", met up with Hosea, the Prophet, whose name meant "Deliverance" because of the sovereign will of God.   Salvation takes place first and then we are complete in Christ as we go on to know the Lord.   The word Salvation means deliverance.   The book of Hosea doesn't tell us whether or not Gomer became a believer of the God of Israel, but it does tell us about God's love for His people in spite of their unfaithfulness.

Let's look at another harlot's life that was completely changed doing Joshua's command.   Rahab, the Harlot, became a woman of God whose life was changed because of her faith when she received the spies and obeyed Joshua's commandment.   (Joshua 2:8-14;6:22-23)   Rahab's faith in the God of Israel made her a woman of God and she married an Israelite named "Salmon."   They had Boaz who married

Ruth who begat Obed; and Obed begat Jesse, and Jesse begat David the King.   Rahab was the great, great- grandmother of David.

Christ Jesus came through the lineage of David, the King; this is why Matthew represented Christ as the "Son" of David.   (Matthew 1:1,5-6; II Samuel 7 chapter)   When we love Elohim with all our heart, soul, and mind He can change our destiny just like He did Rahab.   The spelling of her name in Matthew 1:5 "Rachab" and "Rahab" in Joshua 2:1 is a little different, but if you look up reference to both of these scriptures you will find that they are the same person.

Loving God with all your heart, soul, and might will bring us into the greater blessing of God and that will cause us to receive love and give love to others.   We can have the right-relationships if we learn to love God which is the first and great commandment.   Many hearts have been broken into bits, and pieces.   Fear has gripped the hearts of people instead of love because of past hurts, and made it hard so nothing can come in and nothing can go out.   With the mindset always having our defense mechanism up just in case someone tries to hurt us, and confessing I will never let anyone hurt me again.   Whoever you are reading this book whether you have been molested, rape, or had an unfaithful husband or wife etc., God wants to heal your broken heart.

Isaiah 61:1- "The Spirit of the Lord God is upon me; because the LORD hath anointed me to preach good tidings unto the meek; he hath sent me to bind up the broken-hearted, to proclaim liberty to the captives, and the opening of the prison to them that are bound."
Some men have become womanizers and play games with women emotions never committing themselves to anyone, and visa-versa with the women.   What men and women are doing is setting themselves up for more pain when they play these childish games.   Many have played these games until no one will trust or believe anything they say, and find themselves all alone and that is a pain no one should endure.   Let's look at some examples and see how wrong relationships can affect others and destroy the ones we love.   Look at David and

Bathsheba their relationship caused David, the King, to commit adultery and later he plotted her husband's Uriah's death. If we read David's life we see how God passed judgment against him and it affected his whole family. Some might say I'm not hurting anybody but myself, but this is certainly not true. The song says, "If loving you is wrong I don't want to be right." That song might sound good to the flesh, but it cost too much to sin. (Rom. 6:23) Uriah's life was taken because of David's infidelity. We must realize a little leaven leavens the whole lump. Joseph's brethren hated him so much they plotted to kill him, but God intervened and blessed Joseph instead.

There are many examples in the Bible of wrong relationships and all of us can think of a few relationships that we had and those that went sour in the past. Maybe you are in a wrong relationship right now, and don't know what to do. Pray and ask God to help you and He will guide you in all righteousness. Then go to your Pastor or First lady and asked them to help you.

We must get God on the inside so we can have right relationships with those we care about and love. The first step is to love God. Loving God with all thy heart, soul, and might will cause us to stop playing games. It will bring us into a right relationship with God, and help us love ourselves then we can love our neighbor. Shakespeare wrote, "To thine on-self be true."

If you are a Christian you don't have to find love it's already in your heart. Romans 5:5 "And hope maketh not ashamed; because the love of God is shed abroad in our hearts by the Holy Ghost which is given unto us." If you're not a Christian, Romans 10:9-10 says, "That if thou shalt confess with thy mouth the Lord Jesus, and shalt believe in thine heart that God hath raised him from the dead, thou shalt be saved. 10 For with the heart man believeth unto righteousness; and with the mouth confession is made unto salvation." So you must confess you are a sinner because God said so in Romans 3:23 "All have sinned and come short of the glory of God." Now the next step is to ask him to forgive you and receive Christ Jesus as your Savior.   If you have went through these steps and believe the prayer you prayed you are now a born-again Christian and the angels in heaven are rejoicing.   Welcome to the family of God.

Pray and ask God to put you into a Bible believing Church that preaches Christ and Him crucified.   Do they believe in the Trinity, Healing, Resurrection, Hell, and Heaven.   Here are a few scriptures.   (John 3:3-5; I John 5:7; I Peter 2:24; I Thessalonians 4:13-17; Luke 16:19-31)   If you in our local area and don't have a church home the church address will be in this book.

Author

Barbara L. Brewer Lindsey is an Elder of Haven of Truth Worldwide Deliverance Churches INC. where the Pastors are Apostle Larry N & Co-Pastor Sarah D. Crosby. She is the Author of the Book "Yielding Your Will Totally to God" and writer of the Poem "That's why Jesus Came." Poetry.Com chose and published her poem in a hardbound book with Eternal Portraits alone with other poems from different poets.

May 31, 91 she graduated from Richmond Community College: "Human Services Technology" with an Associate in Applied Science Degree. December 30, 1999 she graduated with honors from Amora Deliverance Theological Institution with a Bachelor of Theology in Pastoral Counseling. April 12, 2011 she graduated with a Master of Theology in Biblical Studies from Amora Deliverance Theological Institution.

She has preached the Gospel since 1983 in the streets and churches and taught the word of God oversees in Frankfurt, Germany. I love to write, preach, and teach the Gospel of Jesus Christ. I have one Son, George F. Brewer, and a daughter-in law, Daisy Brewer.

Sources

Prince, Derek.   God is a Matchmaker.   Copyright © 1986 by
Derek Prince.   Chosen Books Published by Fleming H.
Revell Company Old Tappan, New Jersey

King James Version

New Scorfield Study System.   Editor C.I. SCOFIELD, D.D
New York: Copyright © 1967, 1998 by Oxford University
Press, Inc.

Book Order and Other Information
Available for Revivals, Conventions, and Seminars
Contact: Elder Barbara L. Lindsey
            910-730-4983
  Books: "Yielding Your Will Totally To God"
            "Jesus, Lover, of My Soul"
  Soon to come: "Where Is the Church on God's Prophetic
Calendar?